Edward O. Hinkley, State of Maryland

The Constitution of the State of Maryland

Formed and adopted by the convention which assembled at the city of Annapolis,

May 8, 1867, and submitted to and ratified by the people on the 18th day of

September, 1867

Edward O. Hinkley, State of Maryland

The Constitution of the State of Maryland
Formed and adopted by the convention which assembled at the city of Annapolis, May 8,
1867, and submitted to and ratified by the people on the 18th day of September, 1867

ISBN/EAN: 9783337287153

Printed in Europe, USA, Canada, Australia, Japan

Cover: Foto ©Suzi / pixelio.de

More available books at **www.hansebooks.com**

THE

CONSTITUTION

óf the

STATE OF MARYLAND.

Formed and Adopted by the Convention which Assembled at the City
of Annapolis, May 8, 1867, and Submitted to and Ratified
by the People on the 18th Day of September, 1867.

with

Marginal Notes and References,

To Acts of the General Assembly and Decisions of the Court of Appeals,

And an Appendix and Index.

By EDWARD OTIS HINKLEY, Esq., *of the Baltimore Bar.*

Printed by order of the Convention.

ANNAPOLIS:
WILLIAM THOMPSON, of R.
State Printer.
1868.

Maryland, Sct:

I, GEORGE EARLE, Clerk of the Court of Appeals of Maryland, do hereby certify, that the annexed is a correct copy of the Constitution of Maryland, deposited in the Clerk's Office of said Court, on the seventeenth day of August, in the year of our Lord one thousand eight hundred and sixty-seven.

In Witness whereof, I hereunto set my name as Clerk, and affix the seal of the said Court of Appeals of Maryland on this Twenty-first day of October, eighteen hundred and sixty-seven. GEORGE EARLE, CLERK
of the Court of Appeals of Maryland.

Entered, according to the Act of Congress, in the year 1867, by JOHN MURPHY, in the Clerk's Office of the District Court of Maryland.

PREFACE.

Tuis Edition of the Declaration of Rights and Constitution of Maryland has been prepared in pursuance of an order of the Convention. Great pains have been taken both by the Editor and the Publishers to make it as perfect as possible.

Lists of the Members of the Convention and of its several Committees, and the Proclamations of the Governor convening the Convention, and declaring the adoption of the Constitution by the People have been prefixed.

Notes have been placed on the margin indicating the contents, also notes referring to some of the Acts of Assembly passed since 1851 in pursuance of, or having reference to the Constitutions of 1851 and 1864, and to the Decisions of the Court of Appeals from the foundation of the Government of the State to this date.

A brief commentary is appended shewing the principal changes in the Form of Government of the State, made by the several Constitutions of 1851, 1864 and 1867.

The Index at the end of the work is very full, giving reference to every important word, and the number of the Article, Section and Page wherein it may be found,—and to accomplish this the same matter has been indexed under three or four heads.

It is to be noted that some clerical errors occur in the engrossed document on file in the office of the Clerk of the Court of Appeals,—and the proof having been read by him, so as to make this work as exact as possible, these errors are noted thus: On page 28 the word [of] having been repeated, is placed in brackets in Roman type, and the letter [d] on same page is printed in same way, and on pages 40 and 115, the word [be] having been omitted, is added and placed in brackets. The word *removal* at bottom of page 102, is in the engrossed document, it seems to be an error for *renewal*.

The Publishers have by these additions, as well as by great care in the typography, endeavored to render this edition as accurate as possible. They hope that the Notes, Index, &c., as well as the style in which it is produced will be acceptable to all.

225800   3

PROCEEDINGS.

A PROCLAMATION

By the Governor of Maryland.

State of Maryland, Executive Department.

Whereas, By an Act of the General Assembly of Maryland, passed at January session, 1867, entitled "An Act to provide for taking the sense of the people of this State on the call of a Convention to form a new Constitution and Form of Government, and for assembling the members thereof," it was enacted that an election should be held as provided by said Act to take the sense of the people on the question of the call of the Convention, and to elect delegates thereto in case said call was sustained by a majority of the votes cast;

And Whereas, It is by said Act made the duty of the Governor to count and cast up the number of ballots cast at said election for and against a Convention, and the blank ballots cast, and the ballots cast for delegates to said Convention, and if it should thereupon appear that more votes had been cast in favor of the call of a Convention than against such call, to issue his proclamation declaring the persons having the majority in the several counties and in the city of Baltimore, respectively, to be elected to said Convention, and for the assembling of the members thereof;

And Whereas, The returns of said election have been received from the city of Baltimore and the several counties of the State, and upon counting and casting up the ballots which, according to said returns, were cast at the election held for said purpose on the 10th day of April instant, it appears that the whole number of votes cast was 58,718, of which 34,534 were for a Convention, and 24,136 against a Convention, and 48 blank ballots; and it therefore appearing that

4

more votes have been cast in favor of the call of a Convention than against the call of a Convention—

Now, Therefore, I, THOMAS SWANN, Governor of the State of Maryland, in obedience to the requirements of the Act of Assembly aforesaid, do by this my proclamation declare and make known that the persons having the majority in the several counties and the city of Baltimore, respectively, have been duly elected delegates to said Convention, and that the Convention authorized by said Act will be held in the city of Annapolis, on the SECOND WEDNESDAY OF MAY next, being the eighth day of said month, where the said delegates will, on that day, assemble to enter upon the discharge of the duties prescribed by the Act aforesaid.

 GIVEN under my hand and the Great Seal of the State of Maryland, at the city of Annapolis, this twentieth day of April, in the year of our Lord eighteen hundred and sixty-seven.

THOMAS SWANN.

By the Governor:

JOHN M. CARTER, *Secretary of State.*

In conformity with the aforegoing Proclamation, and in obedience to the requirements of the Act of Assembly, the title of which is therein mentioned, the Convention assembled at 12 o'clock, M., on Wednesday the 8th day of May, in the year one thousand eight hundred and sixty-seven, in the Hall of the House of Delegates, in the city of Annapolis.

All the delegates elect appearing to be present, except Messrs. Thomas I. Hall, of Anne Arundel county, Anthony Kennedy, of Baltimore county, John W. Bennett, of Carroll county, Vivian Brent and John T. Stoddert, of Charles county, James Wallace, of Dorchester county, Henry D. Farnandis, of Harford county, William M. Merrick, of Howard county, and John B. Brooke and Elbert G. Emack, of Prince George's county.

On motion, by Mr. ISAAC D. JONES,

Mr. JOHN F. DENT was appointed temporary President; and Mr. JAMES R. HOWISON, temporary Secretary.

On motion, by Mr. JONES, it was

Ordered, That the Proceedings of the Convention be opened by prayer, and that the Rev. Mr. LEECH, who is now present, be requested to officiate; whereupon,

The Rev. Mr. LEECH offered a prayer.

Mr. CHARLES S. PARRAN, submitted the following order :
Which was agreed to.

Ordered, That a Committee of five be appointed by the Chair to inform the Governor that the Convention to frame a new Constitution for the State of Maryland, has assembled in the Hall of the House of Delegates, in accordance with the Act of the General Assembly, and his Proclamation relating thereto, and has temporarily organized by electing a Chairman and Secretary, and that the Convention desires to have a list of names of the Delegates who are shown by the returns made to him, to have been duly elected members of the Convention ; whereupon,

Messrs. CHARLES S. PARRAN, of Calvert, ISAAC D. JONES, of Somerset, PHILIP H. ROMAN, of Allegany, BERNARD CARTER, of Baltimore city, and J. K. LONGWELL, of Carroll, are appointed the said committee.

The Committee retired, and on returning, reported that they had called on the Governor, as directed by the order of the Convention, and that the Governor would communicate the information desired forthwith.

On motion, by Mr. JONES,
To adjourn until to-morrow, at 12 o'clock,
It was determined in the negative.

The following message was received from the Governor, by Mr. LEARY, his Secretary :

EXECUTIVE DEPARTMENT,
Annapolis, May 8, 1867.

To the Convention :

GENTLEMEN :—In accordance with the application of your Honorable Body through the Committee appointed to confer with me, I transmit herewith a list of the members elected under the Act entitled "An Act to provide for taking the sense of the people of this State on the call of a Convention, to form a new Constitution and Form of Government, and for assembling the members thereof," passed at the late January session of the General Assembly of Maryland : and I also hand you the Proclamation of the Governor issued in accordance with the provisions of the said Act.

The official returns from the several counties and the city of Baltimore are on file in this office, subject to the use of the Convention.

I have the honor to be, with great respect,

Your obedient servant,
THOMAS SWANN.

—•—

Allegany County.

THOMAS PERRY,
ALFRED SPATES,
WILLIAM WALSH,
J. PHILIP ROMAN,
JACOB HOBLITZELL,
THOMAS J. McKAIG.

Anne Arundel County.

JAMES R. HOWISON,
THOMAS I. HALL,
E. G. KILBOURN,
LUTHER GIDDINGS.

Baltimore City—1st Legislative Dist.

LINDSAY H. RENNOLDS,
EZRA WHITMAN,
JOHN H. BARNES,
ISAAC S. GEORGE,
JOSHUA VANSANT,
EDWARD F. FLAHERTY,
JAMES A. HENDERSON.

Baltimore City—2d Legislative Dist.

GEORGE M. GILL,
GEORGE WM. BROWN,
BERNARD CARTER,
ALBERT RITCHIE,
HENRY F. GAREY,
GEORGE W. DOBBIN,
J. HALL PLEASANTS.

Baltimore City—3d Legislative Dist.

JAMES R. BREWER,
JOHN FERRY,
J. MONTGOMERY PETERS,
JOHN FRANCK,
JOS. P. MERRYMAN,
I. M. DENSON,
WALTER S. WILKINSON.

Baltimore County.

CHAS. A. BUCHANAN,
JOHN WETHERED,
EPHRAIM BELL,
ANTHONY KENNEDY,
SAMUEL W. STARR,
CHARLES H. NICOLAI,
ROBERT C. BARRY.

Calvert County.

JOHN PARRAN,
CHARLES S. PARRAN,
JOHN F. IRELAND.

Caroline County.

R. E. HARDCASTLE,
CHAS. E. TARR,
TILGHMAN H. HUBBARD,
W. H. WATKINS.

Carroll County.

JOHN K. LONGWELL,
GEORGE W. MANRO,
STERLING GALT,
BENJ. W. BENNETT,
THOS. F. COVER,
WM. N. HAYDEN.

Cecil County.

BENJ. B. CHAMBERS,
GEORGE R. HOWARD,
JAMES B. GROOME,
JAMES O. McCORMICK,
ELI COSGROVE.

Charles County.

WALTER MITCHELL,
VIVIAN BRENT,
JOHN T. STODDERT.

7

Dorchester County.
JAMES WALLACE,
WM. T. GOLDSBOROUGH,
GEORGE E. AUSTIN,
LEVIN HODSON.

Frederick County.
WILLIAM P. MAULSBY,
FREDERICK J. NELSON,
HARRY W. DORSEY,
OUTERBRIDGE HORSEY,
WILLIAM S. McPHERSON,
JOHN B. THOMAS,
DEWITT C. JOHNSON.

Harford County.
HENRY D. FARNANDIS,
HENRY W. ARCHER,
JOHN EVANS,
EVANS S. ROGERS.
HENRY A. SILVER.

Howard County.
WM. M. MERRICK,
JAMES MACKUBIN,
HENRY O. DEVRIES,
JAMES MORRIS.

Kent County.
JOSEPH A. WICKES,
RICHARD W. RINGGOLD,
C. H. B. MASSEY,
WM. JANVIER.

Montgomery County.
GREENBURY M. WATKINS,
NICHOLAS BREWER,
SAMUEL RIGGS, of R.,
WASHINGTON DUVALL.

Prince George's County.
JOHN F. LEE,
JOHN. B. BROOKE,
FENDALL MARBURY,
ELBERT G. EMACK.

Queen Anne's County.
RICHARD B. CARMICHAEL,
THOMAS J. KEATING,
WASHINGTON FINLEY,
STEPHEN J. BRADLEY.

Saint Mary's County
ROBERT FORD,
JOHN F. DENT,
BAKER A. JAMISON.

Somerset County.
PURNELL TOADVINE,
THOMAS F. J. RIDER,
JAMES L. HORSEY,
ISAAC D. JONES,
HENRY PAGE.

Talbot County.
WILLIAM GOLDSBOROUGH,
RICHARD C. HOLLYDAY,
HENRY E. BATEMAN,
ORMO D HAMMOND.

Washington County.
ANDREW K. SYESTER,
RICHARD H. ALVEY,
JOSEPH MURRAY,
S. S. CUNNINGHAM,
WM. MOTTER,
GEO. POLE.

Worcester County.
J. HOPKINS TARR,
LITTLETON P. FRANKLIN,
THOMAS P. PARKER,
SAMUEL S. McMASTER,
GEORGE W. COVINGTON.

OFFICERS OF THE CONVENTION.

President............ ......Hon. RICHARD B. CARMICHAEL, of Queen Anne's County.

Secretary....................Milton Y. Kidd, of Cecil County.

Assistant Secretary...Thomas H. Moore, of Baltimore County.

Clerk of Revision and Compilation, } Joseph H. Nicholson, of Anne Arundel County.

Sergeant-at-Arms......Charles G. Griffith, of Baltimore City.

Committee Clerks......John V. Posey, of St. Mary's Co.   Stephen P. Toadvine, of Somerset Co.
N. T. Meginnis, of Kent Co., and John H. Woodward, of Baltimore City.

Door Keepers...........John Hagan, of Frederick Co.   Henry Dryden, of Worcester Co.

Postmaster...............J. E. Bateman, of Harford County

STANDING COMMITTEES.

Committee to Consider and Report upon the Declaration of Rights.

Messrs. Jones,	Buchanan,	Austin,	Brooke,
Perry,	Ireland,	Rodgers,	Bradley,
Hall,	Hardcastle,	Morris,	Jamison,
George,	Manro,	Nelson,	Hammond,
Carter,	Howard,	Ringgold,	Syester,
Peters,	Stoddert,	Brewer, of Mont'y,	Parker.

Committee upon the Executive Department.

Messrs. Stoddert,	Vansant,	Wallace,
Perry,	Wethered,	Maulsby,
Hall,	Bennett,	Turr, of Worcester.

Committee upon the Legislative Department.

Messrs. Dent,	Gill,	Howard,
McKaig,	Kennedy,	Farnandis,
Brown,	Hayden,	Page.

Committee upon the Judiciary Department.

Messrs. Dobbin,	Parran, C. S.,	Maulsby,	Keating,
Walsh,	Turr, of Caroline,	Archer,	Ford,
Howison,	Groome,	Mackubin,	Page,
Gill,	Hayden,	Wickes,	Hollyday,
Ritchie,	Brent,	Watkins, of Mont'y,	Motter,
Barry,	Wallace,	Marbury,	Covington.

Committee upon the Attorney-General and State's Attorneys.

Messrs. Barry,	Groome,	Tarr, of Worcester,
Rennolds,	Evans,	Ford,
Garey,	Ringgold,	Archer.

Committee upon the Treasury Department.

Messrs. Hollyday,	Bradley,	Dorsey,
Ferry,	Franklin,	Massey,
Starr,	Chambers,	Emack.

Committee upon the Elective Franchise and the Qualification of Voters.

Messrs. Wickes,   Merryman,   Bateman,
Hoblitzell,   Wethered,   Ford,
Garey,   Duvall,   Syester.

Committee Respecting the Militia and Military Affairs.

Messrs. Lee.   Watkins,   Toadvine,
Giddings,   Wallace,   Pole,
Ferry,   Mackubin,   McMaster.

Committee upon Education.

Messrs. Farnandis,   Bell,   Goldsborough, of Dor.,   Keating,
McKaig,   Parran, Chas. S.,   Johnson,   Jamison,
Kilbourn,   Tarr, of Caroline,   Devries,   Rider,
Vansant,   Cover,   Massey,   Bateman,
Pleasants,   McCormick,   Duvall,   Murray,
Wilkinson,   Brent,   Brooke,   Franklin.

Committee upon a Proper Basis of Representation in the two Houses of the General Assembly, and a Proper Apportionment of Representatives in the Same.

Messrs. Alvey,   Kennedy,   Hodson,   Lee,
Roman,   Parran. John,   Horsey, of Frederick,   Finley,
Giddings,   Hubbard,   Evans,   Dent,
Barnes,   Longwell,   Mackubin,   Toadvine,
Brown,   Cosgrove,   Janvier,   Goldsborough, of
Denson,   Mitchell,   Riggs,   McMaster. [Tal.

Committee Respecting Future Amendments to the Constitution.

Messrs. Maulsby,   Buchanan,   McPherson,
Flaherty,   Archer,   Watkins, of Mon'y,
Franck,   Chambers,   Emack.

Committee Respecting the Appointment, Tenure of Office, Duties and Compensation of all Civil Officers not Embraced in the Duties of Other Standing Committees.

Messrs. Roman,   Mitchell,   Mackubin,
Carter,   Austin,   Lee,
Barry,   McPherson,   Cunningham.

Committee upon Accounts.

Messrs. Howison,   Hubbard,   Dorsey,
Spates,   Chambers,   Riggs,
Whitman,   Janvier,   Silver

Committee upon Printing.

Messrs. Longwell,   Brewer, of Baltimore city,   Dent,
Henderson,   Thomas,   Motter,
Starr,   Silver,   Horsey, of Somerset.

Committee upon Public Works and Corporations.

Messrs. Barnes,   Galt,   Goldsborough, of Dor.,
Spates,   Horsey, of Frederick,   Marbury,
Nicolai,   Farnandis,   McMaster.

Committee on all such Parts of the Constitution as were not Referred to any other Committee.

Messrs. Carter,   Archer,   Mitchell,   Maulsby,   Jones.

Committee on Revision and Compilation.

Messrs. Lee,   Carter,   Farnandis,   Mackubin,   Wickes.

PROCLAMATION BY THE GOVERNOR.

. *Executive Department.*

Whereas, By an Act of the General Assembly of Maryland, passed at January Session, eighteen hundred and sixty-seven, entitled "An Act to provide for taking the sense of the people of this State on the call of a Convention to frame a new Constitution and form of Government, and for assembling the members thereof," it is provided "that the Constitution and form of Government adopted by said Convention shall be submitted to the legal and qualified voters of the State for their adoption or rejection, at such time, in such manner, and subject to such regulations as the said Convention may prescribe."

And Whereas, It is further provided by said act "that the Governor shall receive the returns of the number of votes cast in this State for the adoption or rejection of the Constitution submitted by the Convention to the people of this State, as aforesaid, and upon counting and casting up the returns made to him, as hereinbefore prescribed, if it shall appear that a majority of the votes cast at the said election have been cast in favor of the adoption of the said Constitution, he shall issue his proclamation to the people of the State declaring the fact, and shall take such measures as shall be required by said Constitution to carry the same into effect, and to supersede the existing Constitution."

And Whereas, In pursuance of the said Act, and of a vote of a majority of the people of the State taken in conformity to its provisions, and in favor of the assembling of said Convention, that body did convene at the City of Annapolis on the day appointed by said act, and did on the seventeenth day of August last adopt a new Constitution and form of government, and did therein direct that the same should be submitted to the people of the State for their adoption or rejection, at an election to be held in the city of Baltimore and the various counties for that purpose, on the eighteenth day of September instant.

And Whereas, By said Constitution it is further provided that "the Governor, upon receiving the returns, and ascertaining the aggregate vote throughout the State, shall by his proclamation, make known the

11

same, and if a majority of the votes cast shall be for the adoption of this Constitution, it shall go into effect on Saturday, the fifth day of October, eighteen hundred and sixty-seven."

And Whereas, The returns of said election so held on 'he eighteenth day of September instant have been duly certified to me by the Judges of Election, and upon counting and casting up the same it doth appear that there were forty-seven thousand one hundred and fifty-two (47,152) ballots for the Constitution, and twenty-three thousand and thirty-six (23,036) ballots against the Constitution, and that there were twenty-seven blank ballots; and there being therefore of the aggregate vote so cast a majority in favor of the adoption of said Constitution—

Now, therefore, I, THOMAS SWANN, Governor of the State or Maryland, in pursuance of the authority so vested in me by the said act of Assembly and the Constitution aforesaid, do, by this my proclamation, declare and make known that the said Constitution and form of government so framed and adopted by the Convention aforesaid has been adopted by a majority of the voters of this State, and that in pursuance of the provision therein contained, the same will go into effect as the proper Constitution and form of government of the State, superseding the one now existing, on Saturday, the fifth day of October next.

GIVEN under my hand and the Great Seal of the State of Maryland, at the city of Annapolis, this twenty-seventh day of September, in the year of our Lord one thousand eight hundred and sixty-seven.

THOMAS SWANN.

By the Governor:

JOHN M. CARTER, *Secretary of State.*

Constitution of Maryland,

ADOPTED BY THE CONVENTION,

WHICH ASSEMBLED AT THE CITY OF ANNAPOLIS, ON THE EIGHTH DAY OF MAY, EIGHTEEN HUNDRED AND SIXTY-SEVEN, AND ADJOURNED ON THE SEVENTEENTH DAY OF AUGUST, EIGHTEEN HUNDRED AND SIXTY-SEVEN.

Declaration of Rights.

We, the People of the State of Maryland, grateful to Almighty God for our civil and religious liberty, and taking into our serious consideration the best means of establishing a good Constitution in this State for the sure foundation and more permanent security thereof, declare: — Preamble.

ARTICLE 1. That all Government of right originates from the People, is founded in compact only, and instituted solely for the good of the whole; and they have, at all times, the inalienable right to alter, reform or abolish their Form of Government, in such manner as they may deem expedient. — Origin and Foundation of Government. Right of Reform. 3 Bl. 95; 7 Md. 147; 1861, res. 14.

ART. 2. The Constitution of the United States, and the Laws made, or which shall be made in pursuance thereof, and all Treaties made, or which shall be made, under the — Constitution of U. S.

2   13

authority of the United States, are, and shall

Supreme Law. be the Supreme Law of the State; and the Judges of this State, and all the People of this State, are, and shall be bound thereby;

6 H. & J. 203; 4 G. & J. 1; 3 G. 14; 5 G. 56, 426; 6 G. 200; 2 Md. 457. anything in the Constitution or Law of this State to the contrary notwithstanding.

Powers reserved. ART. 3. The powers not delegated to the United States by the Constitution thereof, nor prohibited by it to the States, are reserved to the States respectively, or to the people thereof.

State's Rights. ART. 4. That the People of this State have the sole and exclusive right of regulating the internal government and police thereof, as a free, sovereign and independent State.

Common Law. ART. 5. That the Inhabitants of Maryland are entitled to the Common Law of England,

Trial by Jury. and the trial by Jury, according to the course of that Law, and to the benefit of such of the

English Statutes. English Statutes as existed on the Fourth day of July, seventeen hundred and seventy-six; and which, by experience, have been found applicable to their local and other circumstances, and have been introduced, used and practiced by the Courts of Law or Equity; and

Acts of Assembly. also of all Acts of Assembly in force on the first day of June, Eighteen hundred and Sixty-seven; except such as may have since expired, or may be inconsistent with the provisions of this Constitution; subject, nevertheless, to the revision of, and amendment or repeal by, the

Charter of the State. Legislature of this State. And the Inhabitants of Maryland are also entitled to all property derived to them from, or under the Charter granted by His Majesty Charles the First to Cæcilius Calvert, Baron of Baltimore. 6. II. & J. 401; 2 G. & J. 254; 6 G & J. 205; 5 G. 45; 2 Md. 429; 7 Md. 135, 416, 500; 16 Md. 549, 539; 15 Md. 548; 1852, c. 60, 275; 1856, c. 220.

ART. 6. That all persons invested with the Legislative or Executive powers of Government are the Trustees of the Public, and, as such, accountable for their conduct: Wherefore, whenever the ends of Government are perverted, and public liberty manifestly endangered, and all other means of redress are ineffectual, the people may, and of right ought, to reform the old, or establish a new Government: the doctrine of non-resistance against arbitrary power and oppression is absurd, slavish and destructive of the good and happiness of mankind. *Right of Reform*

ART. 7. That the right of the people to participate in the Legislature is the best security of liberty and the foundation of all free Government; for this purpose, elections ought to be free and frequent; and every white male citizen, having the qualifications prescribed by the Constitution, ought to have the right of suffrage. *Right of Suffrage. 18 Md. 479.*

ART. 8. That the Legislative, Executive and Judicial powers of. Government ought to be forever separate and distinct from each other; and no. person exercising the functions of one of said Departments shall assume or discharge the duties of any other. *Separation of the Departments of Government. 5 II. & J. 304; 1 G. & J. 463; 1 G. 66; 2 G. 147; 8 G.141; 2 Md.341, 429; 4 Md.189; 9 Md. 526; 10 Md. 478; 15 Md. 376; 18 Md. 193; 22 Md. 183; 4 Md. Ch. 349.*

ART. 9. That no power of suspending Laws or the execution of Laws, unless by, or derived *Suspension of Laws.*

from the Legislature, ought to be exercised, or allowed.

Freedom of Speech. ART. 10. That freedom of speech and debate, or proceedings in the Legislature, ought not to be impeached in any Court of Judicature.

Seat of Government. ART. 11. That Annapolis be the place of meeting of the Legislature; and the Legislature ought not to be convened, or held at any other place but from evident necessity.

Meeting of Legislature. ART. 12. That for redress of grievances, and for amending, strengthening and preserving the Laws, the Legislature ought to be frequently convened.

Right of Petition. ART. 13. That every man hath a right to petition the ·Legislature for the redress of grievances in a peaceable and orderly manner.

Levying of Taxes. ART. 14. That no aid, charge, tax, burthen or fees ought to be rated or levied, under any pretence, without the consent of the Legislature.

Poll Taxes oppressive. ART. 15. That the levying of taxes by the poll is grievous and oppressive, and ought to **Paupers not to be taxed.** be prohibited; that· paupers ought not to be assessed for the support of the Government; but every person in the State, or person holding property therein, ought to contribute his **Taxation according to actual worth.** proportion of public taxes for the support of the Government, according to his actual **Fines, &c.** worth in real or personal property; yet, fines, duties or taxes may properly and justly be imposed, or laid, with a political view for the good government and benefit of the community. 3 H. & M'H. 160; 12 G. & J. 117; 1 G. 302; 2 G. 11, 244, 254, 487; 3 G. 14; 6 G. 290, 1 Md. 368; 7 Md. 1; 12 Md. 195; 18 Md. 1, 451; 20 Md. 516.

ART. 16. That sanguinary Laws ought to be avoided as far as it is consistent with the safety of the State; and no law to inflict cruel and unusual pains and penalties ought to be made in any case, or at any time, hereafter. Sanguinary laws.

ART. 17. That retrospective Laws, punishing acts committed before the existence of such Laws, and by them only declared criminal, are oppressive, unjust and incompatible with liberty; wherefore, no *ex post facto* Law ought to be made; nor any retrospective oath or restriction be imposed, or required. Retrospective Laws.

2 H. & J. 41; 4 G. & J. 1; 12 G. & J. 399; 2 G. 79; 0 G. 302; 1 Md. Ch. 66; 8 Md. 551; 10 Md. 129; 12 Md. 195; 19 Md. 351.

ART. 18. That no Law to attaint particular persons of treason or felony, ought to be made in any case, or at any time, hereafter. Attainder.

ART. 19. That every man, for any injury done to him in his person or property, ought to have remedy by the course of the Law of the Land, and ought to have justice and right, freely without sale, fully without any denial, and speedily without delay, according to the Law of the Land. Right to have justice.
2 Md. 452.

ART. 20. That the trial of facts, where they arise, is one of the greatest securities of the lives, liberties and estate of the People. Trial of Facts where they arise.

ART. 21. That in all criminal prosecutions, every man hath a right to be informed of the Criminal Prosecutions.

Copy of Indictment.

accusation against him; to have a copy of the Indictment, or charge, in due time (if required) to prepare for his defense; to be allowed

Counsel and Witnesses.

counsel; to be confronted with the witnesses against him; to have process for his witnesses; to examine the witnesses for and against him

Trial by Jury. 12 Md. 514.

on oath; and to a speedy trial by an impartial jury, without whose unanimous consent he ought not to be found guilty.

Evidence against oneself. 3 G. 323; 7 Md. 416.

ART. 22. That no man ought to be compelled to give evidence against himself in a criminal case.

Freemen not to be imprisoned. 2 Md. 429.

ART. 23. That no man ought to be taken or imprisoned or disseized of his freehold, liberties or privileges, or outlawed, or exiled, or, in any manner, destroyed, or deprived of his life, liberty or property, but by the judgment of his peers, or by the Law of the Land.

Slavery abolished. 1867, c. 189.

ART. 24. That Slavery shall not be re-established in this State; but having been abolished, under the policy and authority of the United States, compensation, in consideration thereof, is due from the United States.

Bail, Fines, &c.

ART. 25. That excessive bail ought not to be required, nor excessive fines imposed, nor cruel or unusual punishment inflicted, by the Courts of Law.

Search Warrants.

ART. 26. That all warrants, without oath or affirmation, to search suspected places, or to seize any person or property, are grievous and oppressive; and all general warrants to search suspected places, or to apprehend suspected persons, without naming or describing the place, or the person in special, are illegal, and ought not to be granted.

ART. 27. That no conviction shall work corruption of blood or forfeiture of estate. *Corruption of Blood and Forfeiture.*

ART. 28. That a well regulated Militia is the proper and natural defence of a free Government. *Militia.*

ART. 29. That standing Armies are dangerous to liberty, and ought not to be raised, or kept up, without the consent of the Legislature. *Standing Armies.*

ART. 30. That in all cases, and at all times, the military ought to be under strict subordination to, and control of, the civil power. *Military subject to Civil Power.*

ART. 31. That no soldier shall, in time of peace, be quartered in any house, without the consent of the owner, nor in time of war, except in the manner prescribed by Law. *Quartering of Soldiers.*

ART. 32. That no person except regular soldiers, marines, and mariners in the service of this State, or militia, when in actual service, ought, in any case, to be subject to, or punishable by Martial Law. *Martial Law.*

ART. 33. That the independency and uprightness of Judges are essential to the impartial administration of Justice, and a great security to the rights and liberties of the People; Wherefore, the Judges shall not be removed, except in the manner, and for the *Judges.* 14 Md. 216.

causes, provided in this Constitution. No Judge shall hold any other office, civil or military, or political trust, or employment, of any kind, whatsoever, under the Constitution or Laws of this State, or of the United States, or any of them; or receive fees, or perquisites of any kind, for the discharge of his official duties.

1 Md. 368.

Rotation in Office.

ART. 34. That a long continuance in the Executive Departments of power or trust is dangerous to liberty; a rotation therefore, in those Departments is one of the best securities of permanent freedom.

Holding Offices

ART. 35. That no person shall hold, at the same time, more than one office of profit, created by the Constitution or Laws of this State; nor shall any person in public trust receive any present from any foreign Prince or State, or from the United States, or any of them, without the approbation of this State.

Presents.

Religious Liberty.

ART. 36. That as it is the duty of every man to worship God in such manner as he thinks most acceptable to Him, all persons are equally entitled to protection in their religious liberty; wherefore, no person ought, by any Law to be molested in his person or estate, on account of his religious persuasion, or profession, or for his religious practice, unless, under the color of religion, he shall disturb the good order, peace or safety of the State, or shall infringe the laws of morality, or injure others in their natural, civil or religious rights; nor ought any person to be compelled to frequent, or maintain, or contribute, unless on contract, to maintain, any place of worship, or any ministry; nor shall any person, otherwise competent, be deemed incompetent as a witness or juror, on account of Witnesses. his religious belief; provided, he believes in the existence of God, and that under His dispensation such person will be held morally accountable for his acts, and be rewarded or punished therefor either in this world or the world to come.

ART. 37. That no religious test ought ever Oath of Office. to be required as a qualification for any office of profit or trust in this State, other than a declaration of belief in the existence of God; nor shall the Legislature prescribe any other oath of office than the oath prescribed by this Constitution.

ART. 38. That every gift, sale or devise Disqualification of Ministers and Religious bodies from holding certain property. of land, to any Minister, Public Teacher or Preacher of the gospel, as such, or to any Religious Sect, Order or Denomination, or to, or for the support, use or benefit of, or in trust for, any Minister, Public Teacher or Preacher of the gospel, as such, or any Religious Sect, Order or Denomination; and every gift or sale of goods, or chattels, to go in succession, or to take place after the death of the Seller or Donor, to or for such support, use or benefit; and also every devise of goods or chattels to or for the support, use, or benefit of any

Minister, Public Teacher or Preacher of the gospel, as such, or any Religious Sect, Order, or Denomination, without the prior, or subsequent, sanction of the Legislature, shall be void; except always, any sale, gift, lease or devise of any quantity of land, not exceeding five acres, for a church, meeting house, or other house of worship, or parsonage, or for a burying ground, which shall be improved, enjoyed, or used only for such purpose; or such sale, gift, lease, or devise shall be void.

Administering Oaths. ART. 39. That the manner of administering an oath of affirmation to any person, ought to be such as those of the religious persuasion, profession, or denomination, of which he is a member, generally esteem the most effectual confirmation by the attestation of the Divine Being.

Liberty of the Press. ART. 40. That the liberty of the press ought to be inviolably preserved; that every citizen of the State ought to be allowed to speak, write and publish his sentiments on all subjects, being responsible for the abuse of that privilege.

Monopolies. ART. 41. That monopolies are odious, contrary to the spirit of a free government and the principles of commerce, and ought not to be suffered.

Titles of Nobility. ART. 42. That no title of nobility or hereditary honors ought to be granted in this State.

Duties of the Legislature. ART. 43. That the Legislature ought to encourage the diffusion of knowledge and virtue, the extension of a judicious system of general education, the promotion of literature, the arts, sciences, agriculture, commerce and manufactures, and the general melioration of the condition of the People.

Art. 44. That the provisions of the Constitution of the United States, and of this State, apply, as well in time of war, as in time of peace; and any departure therefrom, or violation thereof, under the plea of necessity, or any other plea, is subversive of good Government, and tends to anarchy and despotism. _{Constitutions apply in War and Peace.}

Art. 45. This enumeration of Rights shall not be construed to impair or deny others retained by the People. _{Rights retained by the People. 2 Bl. 99, 209.}

CONSTITUTION.

ARTICLE I.

ELECTIVE FRANCHISE.

Elections by ballot.

Qualifications of Voters.

18 Md. 479.
22 Md. 171.

SECTION 1. All elections shall be by ballot; and every white male citizen of the United States, of the age of twenty-one years, or upwards, who has been a resident of the State for one year, and of the Legislative District of Baltimore City, or of the county, in which he may offer to vote, for six months next preceding the election, shall be entitled to vote, in the ward or election district, in which he resides, at all elections hereafter to be held in this State; and in case any county, or city, shall be so divided as to form portions of different electoral districts, for the election of Representatives in Congress, Senators, Delegates, or other Officers, then, to entitle a person to vote for such officer, he must have been Residence. a resident of that part of the county, or city, which shall form a part of the electoral district, in which he offers to vote, for six months next preceding the election; but a person, who shall have acquired a residence in such county, or city, entitling him to vote at any

such election, shall be entitled to vote in the
election district from which he removed, until _{Removals.}
he shall have acquired a residence in the part
of the county, or city, to which he has removed.

SEC. 2. No person above the age of twenty- _{Disqualifications.}
one years, convicted of larceny, or other in-
famous crime, unless pardoned by the Governor, shall ever thereafter be entitled to vote
at any election in this State; and no person
under guardianship, as a lunatic, or, as a person *non compos mentis,* shall be entitled to vote.

SEC. 3. If any person shall give, or offer to _{Bribery.}
give, directly or indirectly, any bribe, present,
or reward, or any promise, or any security for
the payment, or the delivery of money, or any
other thing, to induce any voter to refrain
from casting his vote, or to prevent him, in
any way, from voting, or to procure a vote for
any candidate, or person proposed, or voted
for, as Elector of President and Vice-Presi-
dent of the United States, or Representative
in Congress, or for any office of profit or trust,
created by the Constitution or Laws of this
State, or by the Ordinances, or Authority of
the Mayor and City Council of Baltimore, the
person giving, or offering to give, and the
person receiving the same, and any person,
who gives, or causes to be given, an illegal
vote, knowing it to be such, at any election
to be hereafter held in this State, shall, on
conviction in a Court of Law, in addition to _{Penalties.}

the penalties now, or hereafter to be, imposed by Law, be forever disqualified to hold any office of profit or trust, or to vote at any election thereafter.

Punishment for Illegal Voting.
1853, c. 133.

Sec. 4. It shall be the duty of the General Assembly to pass Laws to punish, with fine and imprisonment, any person who shall remove into any election district, or precinct of any ward of the City of Baltimore, not for the purpose of acquiring a *bona fide* residence therein, but for the purpose of voting at an approaching election, or, who shall vote in any election district, or ward, in which he does not reside, (except in the case provided for in this article,) or shall, at the same election, vote in more than one election district, or precinct, or shall vote, or offer to vote, in any name not his own, or in place of any other person of the same name, or shall vote in any county, in which he does not reside.

Registration.
1865, c. 159, 174; 1867, c. 336; 1866, res. 3; 1867, c. 17; 22 Md. 176.

Sec. 5. The General Assembly shall provide by Law for a uniform Registration of the names of all the voters in this State, who possess the qualifications prescribed in this Article, which Registration shall be conclusive evidence to the Judges of election of the right of every person, thus registered, to vote at any election thereafter held in this State; but no person shall vote at any election, Federal or State, hereafter to be held in this State, or at any municipal election in the City of Baltimore, unless his name appears in the list of registered voters; and until the General Assembly shall hereafter pass an Act for the Registration of the names of voters, the Law in force on the first day of June, in the year eighteen hundred and sixty-seven, in reference thereto, shall be continued in force, except so far as it may be inconsistent with the provisions of this Constitution; and the registry of voters, made in pursuance thereof, may be corrected, as provided in said Law; but the names of all persons shall be added to the list of qualified voters by the officers of Registration, who have the qualifications prescribed in the first section of this Article, and who are not disqualified under the provisions of the second and third sections thereof.

SEC. 6. Every person elected, or appointed, Oath of Office. to any office of profit or trust, under this Con- 1852, c. 172; 1854, c. 18; 4 Md. 189. stitution, or under the Laws, made pursuant thereto, shall, before he enters upon the duties of such office, take and subscribe the following oath, or affirmation; I, ——, do swear, (or affirm, as the case may be,) that I will support the Constitution of the United States; and that I will be faithful and bear true allegiance to the State of Maryland, and support the Constitution and Laws thereof; and that I will, to the best of my skill and judgment, diligently and faithfully, without partiality or prejudice, execute the office of ——, according to the Constitution and Laws of this State, (and, if a Governor, Senator, Member of the

House of Delegates, or Judge,) that I will not directly or indirectly, receive the profits or any part of the profits, of [of] any other office during the term of my acting as ——.

New Election on Refusal to take Oath.

Sec. 7. Every person, hereafter elected, or appointed, to office, in this State, who shall refuse, or neglect, to take the oath, or affirmation of office, provided for in the sixth section of this Article, shall be considered as having refused to accept the said office; and a new election, or appointment, shall be made, as in case of refusal to accept, or resignation of an office; and any person. violating said oath, shall, on conviction thereof, in a Court of Law, in addition to the penalties now, or hereafter, to be imposed by Law, be thereafter incapable of holding any office of profit or trust in this State.

ARTICLE II.

Executive Department.

Governor's Term of Office. 22 Md. 183.

Section 1. The Executive Power of the State shall be vested in a Governor, whose term of office shall commence on the second Wednesday of January next ensuing his election, and continue for four years, and until his successor shall have qualified; but the Governor chosen[d] at the first election under this Constitution, shall not enter upon the discharge of the duties of the office until the expiration of the term for which the present incumbent was elected; unless the said office shall become vacant by death, resignation, removal from the State, or other disqualification of the said incumbent.

SEC. 2. An election for Governor, under this Constitution, shall be held on the Tuesday next after the first Monday of November, in the year eighteen hundred and sixty-seven, and on the same day and month in every fourth year thereafter, at the places of Voting for Delegates to the General Assembly; and every person qualified to vote for Delegates, shall be qualified and entitled to vote for Governor; the election to be held in the same manner as the election of Delegates, and the returns thereof, under seal, to be addressed to the Speaker of the House of Delegates, and enclosed and transmitted to the Secretary of State, and delivered to said Speaker at the commencement of the session of the General Assembly, next ensuing said election. *Time, place and manner of electing Governor. 1853, c. 134.*

SEC. 3. The Speaker of the House of Delegates shall then open the said Returns, in the presence of both Houses; and the person having the highest number of votes, and being constitutionally eligible, shall be the Governor, and shall qualify, in the manner herein prescribed, on the second Wednesday of January next ensuing his election, or as soon thereafter as may be practicable. *Plurality to elect. 1856, c. 183.*

3

Case of tie Senate and House to choose.

SEC. 4. If two or more persons shall have the highest and an equal number of votes for Governor, one of them shall be chosen Governor by the Senate and House of Delegates; and all questions in relation to the eligibility of Governor, and to the returns of said election, and to the number and legality of votes therein given, shall be determined by the House of Delegates; and if the person, or persons, having the highest number of votes, be ineligible, the Governor shall be chosen by the Senate and House of Delegates. Every election of Governor by the General Assembly shall be determined by a joint majority of the Senate and House of Delegates; and the vote shall be taken *viva voce*. But if two or more persons shall have the highest and an equal number of votes, then, a second vote shall be taken, which shall be confined to the persons having an equal number; and if the vote should again be equal, then the election of Governor shall be determined by lot between those, who shall have the highest and an equal number on the first vote.

House to determine questions of eligibility, &c.

Vote viva voce and jointly.

Case of tie choice by lot.

Qualification of Governor.

SEC. 5. A person to be eligible to the office of Governor, must have attained the age of thirty years, and must have been for ten years a citizen of the State of Maryland, and for five years next preceding his election, a resident of the State, and, at the time of his election, a qualified voter therein.

SEC. 6. In case of the death, or resignation of the Governor, or of his removal from the State, or other disqualification, the General Assembly, if in session, or if not, at their next session, shall elect some other qualified person to be Governor for the residue of the term for which the said Governor had been elected. *In case of death &c. General Assembly to elect.*

SEC. 7. In case of any vacancy in the office of Governor, during the recess of the Legislature, the President of the Senate shall discharge the duties of said office, until a Governor is elected, as herein provided for; and in case of the death or resignation of the said President, or of his removal from the State, or of his refusal to serve, then the duties of said office shall, in like manner, and for the same interval, devolve upon the Speaker of the House of Delegates. And the Legislature may provide by Law, for the impeachment of the Governor; and in case of his conviction, or his inability, may declare what person shall perform the Executive duties; and for any vacancy in said office not herein provided for, provision may be made by Law; and if such vacancy should occur without such provision being made, the Legislature shall be convened by the Secretary of State for the purpose of filling said vacancy. *In case of vacancy during recess President of Senate to act.*

Impeachment.

SEC. 8. The Governor shall be the Commander-in-Chief of the land and naval forces of the State; and may call out the Militia to *Governor to be Commander-in-Chief but not to command in person.*

repel invasions, suppress insurrections, and enforce the execution of the Laws; but shall not take the command in person, without the consent of the Legislature.

His duties. SEC. 9. Hé shall take care that the Laws are faithfully executed.

Appointments.
7 Md. 151.
14 Md. 215. SEC. 10. He shall nominate, and, by and with the advice and consent of the Senate, appoint all civil and military officers of the State, whose appointment, or election, is not otherwise herein provided for; unless a different mode of appointment be prescribed by the Law creating the office.

Appointments
during recess.
2 Md. 341.
14 Md. 215
1862, c. 68. SEC. 11. In case of any vacancy, during the recess of the Senate, in any office which the Governor has power to fill, he shall appoint some suitable person to said office, whose commission shall continue in force until the end of the next session of the Legislature, or until some other person is appointed to the same office, whichever shall first occur; and the nomination of the person thus appointed, during the recess, or, of some other person in his place, shall be made to the Senate within thirty days after the next meeting of the Legislature.

Persons
rejected not to
be appointed. SEC. 12. No person, after being rejected by the Senate, shall be again nominated for the same office at the same session, unless at the request of the Senate; or, be appointed to the same office during the recess of the Legislature.

SEC. 13. All civil officers appointed by the Time of Nomination.
Governor and Senate, shall be nominated to
the Senate within fifty days from the commencement of each regular session of the
Legislature; and their term of office, except
in cases otherwise provided for in this Constitution, shall commence on the first Monday
of May next ensuing their appointment, and
continue for two years (unless removed from
office) and until their successors, respectively,
qualify according to Law; but the term of Term of Office.
office of the Inspectors of Tobacco shall commence on the first Monday of March next
ensuing their appointment.

SEC. 14. If a vacancy shall occur, during Vacancy during Session.
the session of the Senate, in any office which
the Governor and Senate have the power to
fill, the Governor shall nominate to the Senate
before its final adjournment, a proper person
to fill said vacancy, unless such vacancy
occurs within ten days before said final adjournment.   ·

SEC. 15. The Governor may suspend, or Courts Martial.
14 Md. 215.
arrest any military officer of the State for dis-
obedience of orders, or other military offence;
and may remove him in pursuance of the
sentence of a Court Martial; and may remove
for incompetency, or misconduct, all civil
officers who received appointment from the
Executive for a term of years.

SEC. 16. The Governor shall convene the Extra Sessions of Legislature.
Legislature, or the Senate alone, on extraor-

dinary occasions; and whenever from the presence of an enemy, or from any other cause, the Seat of Government shall become an unsafe place for the meeting of the Legislature, he may direct their sessions to be held at some other convenient place.

Veto power.   SEC. 17. To guard against hasty or partial legislation, and encroachments of the Legislative Department upon the co-ordinate Executive and Judicial Departments, every Bill which shall have passed the House of Delegates and the Senate, shall, before it becomes a Law, be presented to the Governor of the State; if he approve, he shall sign it; but if not, he shall return it, with his objections, to the House in which it originated, which House shall enter the objections at large on its Journal, and proceed to re-consider the Bill; if, after such re-consideration, three-fifths of the members elected to that House shall pass the Bill, it shall be sent, with the objections to the other House, by which it shall likewise be re-considered, and if passed by three-fifths of the members elected to that House, it shall become a Law. But, in all such cases, the votes of both Houses shall be determined by yeas and nays; and the names of the persons voting for and against the Bill, shall be entered on the Journal of each House, respectively. If any Bill shall not be returned by the Governor within six days, (Sundays excepted) after it shall have been presented

Three-fifths of each House may pass a vetoed bill.

Yeas and Nays.

Veto within six days.

to him, the same shall be a Law in like
manner as if he signed it; unless the General Assembly shall, by adjournment, prevent its return, in which case it shall not be
a Law.

Sec. 18. It shall be the duty of the Gov- Governor to
examine Trea-
ernor, semi-annually (and oftener, if he deem sury accounts.
it expedient) to examine under oath the Treasurer and Comptroller of the State on all matters pertaining to their respective offices; and
inspect and review their Bank and other Account Books.

Sec. 19. He shall, from time to time, in- Recommendations.
form the Legislature of the condition of the
State and recommend to their consideration
such measures as he may judge necessary
and expedient.

Sec. 20. He shall have power to grant Pardoning
power.
reprieves and pardons, except in cases of impeachment, and in cases, in which he is prohibited by other Articles of this Constitution;
and to remit fines and forfeitures for offences
against the State; but shall not remit the
principal, or interest of any debt due the
State, except, in cases of fines and forfeitures;
and before granting a *nolle prosequi*, or par-
don, he shall give notice, in one or more Notice in newspapers.
newspapers, of the application made for it,
and of the day on, or after which, his decision will be given; and in every case, in
which he exercises this power, he shall re- Reports to
Legislature.
port to either Branch of the Legislature,

whenever required, the petitions, recommendations, and reasons, which influenced his decision.

Residence and
Salary.

SEC. 21. The Governor shall reside at the Seat of Government, and receive for his services an annual salary of Four Thousand Five Hundred dollars.

A Secretary of
State.
1853, c. 448.
1858, c. 32.

SEC. 22. A Secretary of State shall be appointed by the Governor, by and with the advice and consent of the Senate, who shall continue in office, unless sooner removed by the Governor, till the end of the official term of the Governor from whom he received his appointment, and receive an annual salary of Two Thousand dollars, and shall· reside at the Seat of Government; and the office of Private Secretary shall thenceforth cease.

His duties.

SEC. 23. The Secretary of State shall carefully keep and preserve a Record of all official acts and proceedings, which may at all times be inspected by a committee of ·either Branch of the Legislature; and he shall perform such other duties as may be prescribed by Law, or as may properly belong to his office, together with all clerical duty belonging to the Executive Department.

ARTICLE III.

LEGISLATIVE DEPARTMENT.

SECTION 1. The Legislature shall consist of two distinct Branches; a Senate, and a House of Delegates, and shall be styled the General Assembly of Maryland. *Two Branches* *Style.*

SEC. 2. Each County in the State, and each of the three Legislative Districts of Baltimore City, as they are now, or may hereafter be defined, shall be entitled to one Senator, who shall be elected by the qualified voters of the Counties, and of the Legislative Districts of Baltimore City, respectively, and shall serve for four years from the date of his election, subject to the classification of Senators, hereafter provided for. *Election of Senators.* *Term four years.*

SEC. 3. Until the taking and publishing of the next National Census, or until the enumeration of the population of this State, under the Authority thereof, the several Counties, and the City of Baltimore, shall have representation in the House of Delegates, as follows: Alleghany County, five Delegates; Anne Arundel County, three Delegates; Baltimore County, six Delegates; each of the three Legislative Districts of the City of Baltimore, six Delegates; Calvert County, two Delegates; Caroline County, two Delegates; Carroll County, four Delegates; Cecil County, *Representation in House of Delegates until next Census.*

four Delegates; Charles County, two Delegates; Dorchester County, three Delegates; Frederick County, six Delegates; Harford County, four Delegates; Howard County, two Delegates; Kent County, two Delegates; Montgomery County, three Delegates; Prince George's County, three Delegates; Queen Anne's County, two Delegates; Saint Mary's County, two Delegates; Somerset County, three Delegates; Talbot County, two Delegates; Washington County, five Delegates; and Worcester County, three Delegates.

Basis of Representation in House of Delegates.

SEC. 4. As soon as may be after the taking and publishing of the next National Census, or after the enumeration of the population of this State, under the Authority thereof, there shall be an apportionment of representation in the House of Delegates, to be made on the following basis, to wit: Each of the several Counties of the State, having a population of eighteen thousand souls, or less, shall be entitled to two Delegates; and every County, having a population of over eighteen thousand, and less than twenty-eight thousand souls, shall be entitled to three Delegates; and every County, having a population of twenty-eight thousand, and less than forty thousand souls, shall be entitled to four Delegates; and every County, having a population of forty thousand, and less than fifty-five thousand souls, shall be entitled to five Delegates; and every County, having a population

of fifty-five thousand souls, and upwards,
shall be entitled to six Delegates, and no
more; and each of the three Legislative Districts of the City of Baltimore shall be entitled to the number of Delegates to which the
largest County shall, or may be entitled,
under the aforegoing apportionment. And
the General Assembly shall have power to Legislative Districts in
provide by Law, from time to time, for alter- Baltimore City may bo changed.
ing and changing the boundaries of the three
existing Legislative Districts of the City of
Baltimore, so as to make them, as near as
may be, of equal population; but said Districts shall always consist of contiguous territory.

SEC. 5. Immediately after the taking and Governor to arrange the
publishing of the next National Census, or Representation in House.
after any State enumeration of population,
as aforesaid, it shall be the duty of the Governor, then being, to arrange the Representation in said House of Delegates, in accordance
with the apportionment herein provided for;
and to declare, by Proclamation, the number Proclamation.
of Delegates, to which each County, and the
City of Baltimore may be entitled, under such
apportionment; and after every National Census taken thereafter, or after any State enumeration of population, thereafter made, it
shall be the duty of the Governor, for the
time being, to make similar adjustment of
Representation, and to declare the same by
Proclamation, as aforesaid.

Election of Delegates.

SEC. 6. The members of the House of Delegates shall be elected by the qualified voters of the Counties, and the Legislative Districts of Baltimore City, respectively, to serve for two years, from the day of their election.

Term two years.

Time of Elections.

SEC. 7. The first election for Senators and Delegates shall take place on the Tuesday next, after the first Monday in the month of November, eighteen hundred and sixty-seven; and the election for Delegates, and as nearly as practicable, for one-half of the Senators, shall be held on the same day, in every second year thereafter.

Classification of Senators.

SEC. 8. Immediately after the Senate shall have convened, after the first election, under this Constitution, the Senators shall be divided by lot, into two classes, as nearly equal in number as may be—Senators of the first class shall go out of office at the expiration of two years, -and Senators shall be elected on the Tuesday next after the first Monday in the. month of November, eighteen hundred and sixty-nine, for the term of four years, to supply their places; so that, after the first election, one-half of the Senators may be chosen every second year. In case the number of Senators be hereafter increased, such classification of the additional Senators shall be made as to preserve, as nearly as may be, an equal number in each class.

Qualifications of Senators and Delegates.
4 H. & M'H. 279.

SEC. 9. No person shall [be] eligible as a Senator or Delegate, who at the time of his

·election, is not a citizen of the State of Maryland, and who has not resided therein, for at
least three years, next preceding the day of
his election, and the last year thereof, in the
County, or in the Legislative District of Baltimore City, which he may be chosen to represent, if such County, or Legislative District of said City, shall have been so long
established; and if not, then in the County,
or City, from which, in whole, or in part,
the same may have been formed; nor shall
any person be eligible as a Senator, unless
he shall have attained the age of twenty-five
years, nor as a Delegate, unless he shall have
attained the age of twenty-one years, at the
time of his election.   ·

SEC. 10. No member of Congress, or person   Persons ineligible.
holding any civil or military office under the 1853, c. 280.
United States, shall be eligible as a Senator,
or Delegate; and if any person shall after his
election as Senator, or Delegate, be elected
to Congress, or be appointed to any office,
civil, or military, under the Government of
the United States, his acceptance thereof, shall
vacate his seat.

SEC. 11. No Minister or Preacher of the
Gospel, or of any religious creed, or denomi-
nation, and no person holding any civil office
of profit, or trust, under this State, except
Justices of the Peace, shall be eligible as
Senator, or Delegate.

SEC. 12. No Collector, Receiver, or Holder   Defaulters
ineligible.
of public money shall be eligible as Senator   1856, c. 16.

or Delegate, or to any office of profit, or trust, under this State, until he shall have accounted for, and paid into the Treasury all sums on the Books thereof charged to, and due by him.

SEC. 13. In case of death, disqualification, resignation, refusal to act, expulsion, or removal from the county, or city, for which he shall have been elected, of any person, who shall have been chosen as a Delegate, or Senator, or in case of a tie between two or more such qualified persons, a warrant of election shall be issued by the Speaker of the House of Delegates, or President of the Senate, as the case may be, for the election of another person in his place, of which election, not less than ten days notice shall be given, exclusive of the day of the publication of the notice, and of the day of election; and, if during the recess of the Legislature, and more than ten days before its termination, such death shall occur, or such resignation, refusal to act, or disqualification be communicated, in writing to the Governor by the person, so resigning, refusing, or disqualified, it shall be the duty of the Governor to issue a warrant of election to supply the vacancy thus created, in the same manner, the said Speaker, or President, might have done, during the session of the General Assembly; provided, however, that unless a meeting of the General Assembly may intervene, the election, thus ordered to fill such vacancy, shall be held on the day of the ensuing election for Delegates and Senators.

SEC. 14. The General Assembly shall meet *Meetings of Legislature.* on the first Wednesday of January, eighteen hundred and sixty-eight, and on the same day in every second year thereafter, and at no other time, unless convened by proclamation of the Governor.

SEC. 15. The General Assembly may continue its Session so long as, in its judgment *Compensation of Members. 1864, res. 4.* the public interest may require, for a period not longer than ninety days; and each member thereof, shall receive a compensation of five dollars per diem, for every day he shall attend the session; but not for such days as he may be absent, unless absent on account of sickness, or by leave of the House of which he is a member; and he shall also receive such mileage as may be allowed by Law, not exceeding twenty cents per mile; and the Presiding officer of each House shall receive an additional compensation of three dollars per day. When the General Assembly shall be convened by Proclamation of *Extra Sessions.* the Governor, the session shall not continue longer than thirty days; and in such case, the compensation shall be the same as herein prescribed.

SEC. 16. No book, or other printed matter, *Books not to be purchased.* not appertaining to the business of the session, shall be purchased, or subscribed for, for the use of the members of the General Assembly, or be distributed among them, at the public expense.

Disqualifications to hold certain offices.

SEC. 17. No Senator or Delegate, after qualifying as such, notwithstanding he may thereafter resign, shall during the whole period of time, for which he was elected, be eligible to any office, which shall have been created, or the salary, or profits of which shall have been increased, during such term.

Exemption for words in debate.

SEC. 18. No Senator, or Delegate shall be liable in any civil action, or criminal prosecution, whatever, for words spoken in debate.

Powers of each House

SEC. 19. Each House shall be judge of the qualifications and elections of its members, as prescribed by the Constitution and Laws of the State; shall appoint its own officers, determine the rules of its own proceedings, punish a member for disorderly or disrespectful behaviour, and with the consent of two-thirds of its whole number of members elected, expel a member; but no member shall be expelled a second time for the same offence.

Quorum.

SEC. 20. A majority of the whole number of members elected to each House shall constitute a quorum for the transaction of business; but a smaller number may adjourn from day to day, and compel the attendance of absent members, in such manner, and under such penalties, as each House may prescribe.

Sessions to be open.

SEC. 21. The doors of each House, and of the Committee of the Whole, shall be open, except when the business is such as ought to be kept secret.

Sec. 22. Each House shall keep a Journal of its proceedings, and cause the same to be published. The yeas and nays of members on any question, shall at the call of any five of them in the House of Delegates, or one in the Senate, be entered on the Journal. *Journals to be published.*

Yeas and Nays 1853, c. 36.

Sec. 23. Each House may punish by imprisonment, during the session of the General Assembly, any person, not a member, for disrespectful, or disorderly behaviour in its presence, or for obstructing any of its proceedings, or any of its officers in the execution of their duties; provided, such imprisonment shall not, at any one time, exceed ten days. *Imprisonment of disorderly persons.*

Sec. 24. The House of Delegates may inquire, on the oath of witnesses, into all complaints, grievances and offences, as the Grand Inquest of the State, and may commit any person, for any crime, to the public jail, there to remain, until discharged by due course of Law. They may examine and pass all accounts of the State, relating either to the collection or expenditure of the revenue, and appoint Auditors to state and adjust the same. They may call for all public, or official papers and records, and send for persons, whom they may judge necessary, in the course of their inquiries, concerning affairs relating to the public interest, and may direct all office bonds which shall be made payable to the State, to be sued for any breach thereof; and with the view to the more certain pre- *Powers of the House of Delegates.*

Grand Inquest

Send for persons and papers. 7 Md. 466.

4

vention, or correction of the abuses in the
expenditures of the money of the State, the
General Assembly shall create, at every session thereof, a joint Standing Committee of
the Senate and House of Delegates, who shall
have power to send for persons, and examine
them on oath, and call for Public, or Official
Papers and Records, and whose duty it shall

Contracts. be to examine and report upon all contracts
made for printing, stationery, and purchases
for the Public offices, and the Library, and
all expenditures therein, and upon all matters

Abuse in
expenditures. of alleged abuse in expenditures, to which
their attention may be called by Resolution
of either House of the General Assembly.

Special
adjournments. SEC. 25. Neither House shall, without the
consent of the other, adjourn for more than
three days, at any one time, nor adjourn to
any other place, than that in which the House
shall be sitting, without the concurrent vote
of two-thirds of the members present.

Impeachment. SEC. 26. The House of Delegates shall have
the sole power of impeachment in all cases;
but a majority of all the members elected
must concur in the impeachment. All im-
peachments shall be tried by the Senate, and
when sitting for that purpose, the Senators
shall be on oath, or affirmation, to do justice
according to the law and the evidence; but
no person shall be convicted without the concurrence of two-thirds of all the Senators
elected.

SEC. 27. Any bill may originate in either House of the General Assembly, and be altered, amended, or rejected by the other; but no bill shall originate in either House during the last ten days of the session, unless two-thirds of the members elected thereto shall so determine by yeas and nays; nor shall any bill become a Law, until it be read on three different days of the ·session in each House, unless two-thirds of the members elected to the House, where such bill is pending, shall so determine by yeas and nays; and no bill shall be read a third time until it shall have been actually engrossed for a third reading. *Either House may originate bills.*

SEC. 28. No bill shall become a Law unless it be passed in each House by a majority of the whole number of members elected, and on its final passage, the yeas and nays be recorded; nor shall any Resolution, requiring the action of both Houses, be passed except in the same manner. *Passage of Bills.*

SEC. 29. The style of all Laws of this State shall be, "Be it enacted by the General Assembly of Maryland:" and all Laws shall be passed by original bill; and every Law enacted by the General Assembly shall embrace but one subject, and that shall be described in its title; and no Law, nor section of Law, shall be revived, or amended by reference to its title, or section only; nor shall any Law be construed by reason of its *Style of Laws.* *Mode of enactment.* *7 Md. 151; 1852, res. 14; 11 Md. 525; 14 Md. 184; 22 Md. 126.*

title, to grant powers, or confer rights which are not expressly contained in the body of the Act; and it shall be the duty of the General Assembly, in amending any article, or section of the Code of Laws of this State, to enact the same, as the said article, or section would read when amended. And whenever the General Assembly shall enact any Public General Law, not amendatory of any section, or article in the said Code, it shall be the duty of the General Assembly to enact the same, in articles and sections, in the same manner, as the Code is arranged, and to provide for the publication of all additions and alterations, which may be made to the said Code.

Bills to be sign-
ed by Governor
and recorded in
Court of Ap-
peals.
14 Md. 184.

SEC. 30. Every bill, when passed by the General Assembly, and sealed with the Great Seal, shall be presented to the Governor, who, if he approves it, shall sign the same in the presence of the presiding officers and Chief Clerks of the Senate and House of Delegates. Every Law shall be recorded in the office of the Court of Appeals, and in due time, be printed, published and certified under the Great Seal, to the several Courts, in the same manner as has been heretofore usual in this State.

When laws take
effect.
14 Md. 184; 19
Md. 96; 1865, c.
31.

SEC. 31. No Law passed by the General Assembly shall take effect, until the first day of June, next after the Session, at which it may be passed, unless it be otherwise expressly declared therein.

SEC. 32. No money shall be drawn from Appropriations to be made by law. 4 Md. 189. the Treasury of the State, by any order or resolution, nor except in accordance with an appropriation by Law, and every such Law shall distinctly specify the sum appropriated, and the object, to which it shall be applied; provided, that nothing herein contained shall prevent the General Assembly from placing a contingent fund at the disposal of the Execu- Contingent Fund. tive, who shall report to the General Assem- 1854, c. 16. bly, at each Session, the amount expended, and the purposes to which it was applied. An accurate statement of the receipts and expenditures of the public money, shall be attached to, and published with the Laws, after each regular Session of the General Assembly.

SEC. 33. The General Assembly shall not Local and special laws not to be passed. pass local, or special Laws, in any of the fol- 1 H. & J. 236; 3 lowing enumerated cases, viz: For extending H. & J. 2, 43, 302; 1 G. & J. 463; 6 G. & J. 461; 7 G. the time for the collection of taxes; granting & J. 7, 191; 8 G. & J. 386; 9 G. & divorces; changing the name of any person; J. 365; 11 G. & J. 87; 12 G. & J. 257, providing for the sale of real estate belonging 286, 400; 2 Bl. 209; 2 Md. 429. to minors, or other persons laboring under legal disabilities, by executors, administrators, guardians or trustees; giving effect to informal, or invalid deeds or wills; refunding money paid into the State Treasury, or releasing persons from their debts, or obligations to the State, unless recommended by the Governor, or officers of the Treasury Department. And the General Assembly shall pass no special Law, for any case; for which provision has been made, by an existing General Law. The General Assembly, at its first session after the adoption of this Constitution,

General Laws to be provided. shall pass General Laws, providing for the cases enumerated in this section, which are not already adequately provided for, and for all other cases, where a General Law can be made applicable.

Debts not to be contracted. SEC. 34. No debt shall be hereafter contracted by the General Assembly, unless such debt shall be authorized by a Law, providing for the collection of an annual tax, or taxes, sufficient to pay the interest on such debt, as it falls due; and also, to discharge the principal thereof, within fifteen years from the time of contracting the same; and the taxes, laid for this purpose, shall not be repealed, or applied to any other object, until the said debt, and interest thereon, shall be fully dis-

Credit of the State not to be given. 15 Md. 205. charged. The credit of the State shall not in any manner be given, or loaned to, or in aid of any individual, association, or corporation; nor shall the General Assembly have the power, in any mode, to involve the State in the construction of Works of Internal Improvement, nor in granting any aid thereto, which shall involve the faith, or credit of the State; nor make any appropriation therefor, except in aid of the construction of Works of Internal Improvement, in the counties of Saint Mary's, Charles and Calvert, which have had

no direct advantage, from such Works, as have
been heretofore aided by the State; and provided, that such aid, advances, or appropriations shall not exceed in the aggregate the
sum of five hundred thousand dollars. And
they shall not use, or appropriate the pro-
ceeds of the Internal Improvement Companies, or of the State tax, now levied, or which
may hereafter be levied, to pay off the public *Public Debt of the State.*
debt, to any other purpose until the interest
and debt are fully paid, or the sinking fund
shall be equal to the amount of the outstand-
ing debt; but the General Assembly may,
without laying a tax, borrow an amount never
to exceed fifty thousand dollars, to meet tem- *Temporary deficiencies.*
porary deficiencies in the Treasury, and may
contract debts to any amount that may be
necessary for the defence of the State.

SEC. 35. No extra compensation shall be *Extra compensation not to be allowed.*
granted, or allowed by the General Assembly,
to any Public Officer, Agent, Servant or Con-
tractor, after the service shall have been rendered, or the contract entered into; nor shall.
the salary, or compensation of any public
officer be increased, or diminished during his
term of office.

SEC. 36. No Lottery grant shall ever here- *Lotteries prohibited.*
after be authorized by the General Assembly. *12 G. & J. 1.*

SEC. 37. The General Assembly shall pass *Payment for Slaves prohibited.*
no Law providing for payment, by this State,
for Slaves emancipated from servitude in this
State; but they shall adopt such measures, as

they may deem expedient, to obtain from the United States, compensation for such Slaves, and to receive, and distribute the same, equitably, to the persons entitled.

No imprison-
ment for Debt.
5 Md. 337.
6 Md. 308.

SEC. 38. No person shall be imprisoned for debt.

Banks.
1853, c. 441.
1854, c. 152.

SEC. 39. The General Assembly shall grant no charter for Banking purposes, nor renew any Banking Corporation, now in existence, except upon the condition that the Stockholders shall be liable to the amount of their respective Share, or Shares of Stock in such Banking Institution, for all its debts and liabilities, upon note, bill, or otherwise; the

Books to be
open.

Books, papers, and accounts of all Banks shall be open to inspection, under such regulations as may be prescribed by Law.

Compensation
for property
taken for Pub-
lic use.
4 G. & J. 1; 9 G.
& J. 479; 2 G. 20;
5 G. 383; 2 Bl.
99, 673; 3 Bl. 95,
386, 453; 1 Md.
Ch. 107, 248; 1
Md. 553; 5 Md.
237, 314: 7 Md.
500; 10 Md. 544:
14 Md. 444; 15
Md. 193, 240; 22
Md. 229; 1853, c.
179.

SEC. 40. The General Assembly shall enact no Law authorizing private property, to be taken for public use, without just compensation, as agreed upon between the parties, or awarded by a jury, being first paid, or tendered to the party, entitled to such compensation.

Duellists
ineligible.

SEC. 41. Any citizen of this State, who shall after the adoption of this Constitution, either in, or out of this State, fight a duel with deadly weapons, or send, or accept a challenge so to do, or who shall act as a second, or knowingly aid or assist in any manner, those offending, shall, ever thereafter, be incapable of holding any office of profit or trust, under this State, unless relieved from the disability by an act of the Legislature.

SEC. 42. The General Assembly shall pass Laws necessary for the preservation of the purity of Elections. *Purity of Elections.*

SEC. 43. The property of the wife shall be protected from the debts of her husband. *Wife's property protected. 12 Md. 294; 19 Md. 9; 1853, c. 245, 335.*

SEC. 44. Laws shall be passed by the General Assembly, to protect from execution a reasonable amount of the property of the debtor, not exceeding in value, the sum of five hundred dollars. *Exemption Laws.*

SEC. 45. The General Assembly shall provide a simple and uniform system of charges in the offices of Clerks of Courts, and Registers óf Wills, in the Counties of this State, and the City of Baltimore, and for the collection thereof; provided, the amount of compensation to any of the said officers, in the various Counties, shall not exceed the sum of three thousand dollars a year, and in the City of Baltimore thirty-five hundred dollars a year, over and above office expenses, and compensation to assistants; and provided further, that such compensation, of Clerks, Registers, assistants and office expenses shall always be paid out of the fees, or receipts of the offices, respectively. *Compensation to Clerks and Registers. 1852, c. 308.*

SEC. 46. The General Assembly shall have power to receive from the United States, any grant, or donation of land, money, or securities for any purpose designated by the United *Legislature may receive land from U. S.*

States, and shall administer, or distribute the same according to the conditions of the said grant.

Contested
Elections.
17 Md. 309.
1853, c. 244.
SEC. 47. The General Assembly shall make provisions for all cases of contested elections of any of the officers, not herein provided for.

Corporations
to be formed
under gene-
ral laws.
1852, c. 231; 1853,
c. 320; 1854, c.
147; 1867, c. 379.
SEC. 48. Corporations may be formed under general Laws; but shall not be created by special act, except for municipal purposes, and except in cases, where no general Laws exist, providing for the creation of corporations of the same general character, as the corporation proposed to be created; and any act of incorporation, passed in violation of this section shall be void. And as soon as practicable, after the adoption of this Constitution, it shall be the duty of the Governor, to appoint three persons learned in the Law, whose duty it shall be, to prepare drafts of general Laws, providing for the creation of corporations, in such cases as may be proper, and for all other cases, where a general Law can be made; and for revising and amending, so far as may be necessary, or expedient, the general Laws which may be in existence on the first day of June, eighteen hundred and sixty-seven, providing for the creation of corporations, and for other purposes; and such
Commissioners
to revise laws.
drafts of Laws shall by said commissioners, be submitted to the General Assembly, at its first meeting, for its action thereon; and each of said commissioners shall receive a com-

pensation of five hundred dollars for his services, as such commissioner.

All Charters granted, or adopted, in pursuance of this section, and all Charters heretofore granted and created, subject to repeal or modification, may be altered, from time to time, or be repealed; provided, nothing herein contained shall be construed to extend to Banks, or the incorporation thereof. Charters may be repealed.

SEC. 49. The General Assembly shall have power to regulate by Law, not inconsistent with this Constitution, all matters which relate to the Judges of election, time, place and manner of holding elections in this State, and of making returns thereof. Regulation of Elections.

SEC. 50. It shall be the duty of the General Assembly, at its first session, held after the adoption of this Constitution, to provide by Law for the punishment, by fine, or imprisonment in the Penitentiary, or both, in the discretion of the Court, of any person, who shall bribe, or attempt to bribe, any Executive, or Judicial officer of the State of Maryland, or any member, or officer of the General Assembly of the State of Maryland, or of any Municipal Corporation in the State of Maryland, or any Executive officer of such corporation, in order to influence him in the performance of any of his official duties; and, also, to provide by Law for the punishment, by fine, or imprisonment in the Penitentiary, or both, in the discretion of the Court, of Bribery. Punishment.

Evidence.

any of said officers, or members, who shall demand, or receive any bribe, fee, reward, or testimonial, for the performance of his official duties, or for neglecting, or failing to perform the same; and, also, to provide by Law for compelling any person, so bribing, or attempting to bribe, or so demanding, or receiving a bribe, fee, reward, or testimonial, to testify against any person, or persons, who may have committed any of said offences; provided, that any person, so compelled to testify, shall be exempted from trial and punishment for the offence, of which he may have been guilty; and any person, convicted of such offence, shall, as part of the punishment thereof, be

Disqualification.

forever disfranchised and disqualified from holding any office of trust, or profit, in this State.

Taxation of personal property.

SEC. 51. The personal property of residents of this State, shall be subject to taxation in the county, or city, where the resident *bona fide* resides for the greater part of the year, for which the tax may, or shall be levied, and not elsewhere, except goods and chattels permanently located, which shall be taxed in the City, or County where they are so located.

Appropriations for private claims.

SEC. 52. The General Assembly shall appropriate no money out of the Treasury for payment of any private claim against the State exceeding three hundred dollars, unless said claim shall have been first presented to the Comptroller of the Treasury, together

with the proofs upon which the same is
founded, and reported upon by him.

Sec. 53. No person shall be incompetent, Witness. Race or Color.
as a witness, on account of race or color,
unless hereafter so declared by Act of the
General Assembly.

Sec. 54. No County of this State shall con- No County to contract debt unless authorized.
tract any debt, or obligation, in the construc-
tion of any Railroad, Canal, or other Work of
Internal Improvement, nor give, or loan its
credit to, or in aid of any association, or corporation, unless authorized by an Act of the
General Assembly, which shall be published
for two months before the next election for
members of the House of Delegates in the
newspapers published in such County, and
shall also be approved by a majority of all
the members elected to each House of the
General Assembly at its next Session after
said election.

Sec. 55. The General Assembly shall pass Habeas Corpus.
no Law suspending the privilege of the Writ
of *Habeas Corpus.*

Sec. 56. The General Assembly shall have Laws to execute vested powers.
power to pass all such Laws as may be neces-
sary and proper for carrying into execution
the powers vested, by this Constitution, in any
Department, or office of the Government, and
the duties imposed upon them thereby.

Sec. 57. The Legal Rate of Interest shall be Rate of Interest. 13 Md. 202.
six per cent. per annum; unless otherwise pro-
vided by the General Assembly.

Foreign Corporations to be taxed.

Sec. 58. The Legislature at its first session after the ratification of this Constitution shall provide by Law for State and municipal taxation upon the revenues accruing from business done in the State by all foreign corporations.

Pension system abolished.

Sec. 59. The office of "State Pension Commissioner" is hereby abolished; and the Legislature shall pass no law creating such . office, or establishing any general pension system within this State.

ARTICLE IV.

Judiciary Department.

Part I—General Provisions.

The Judicial Power how vested.
8 Md. 227; 17 Md. 331; 22 Md. 491.

Section 1. The Judicial power of this State shall be vested in a Court of Appeals, Circuit Courts, Orphans' Courts, such Courts for the City of Baltimore as are hereinafter provided for, and Justices of the Peace; all said Courts

Courts of Record.

shall be Courts of Record, and each shall have a seal to be used in the authentication of all process issuing therefrom. The process

Justices of the Peace.

and official character of Justices of the Peace shall be authenticated as hath heretofore been practiced in this State, or may hereafter . be prescribed by Law.

SEC. 2. The Judges of all of the said Courts _{Qualifications of Judges.} shall be citizens of the State of Maryland, and qualified voters under this Constitution, and shall have resided therein not less than five years, and not less than six months next preceding their election, or appointment, in the Judicial Circuit, as the case may be, for which they may be, respectively, elected, or appointed. They shall be not less than thirty years of age at the time of their election, or appointment, and shall be selected from those who have been admitted to practice Law in this State, and who are most distinguished for integrity, wisdom and sound legal knowledge.

SEC. 3. The Judges of the said several Courts shall be elected in the Counties by the qualified voters in their respective Judicial Circuits, as hereinafter provided, at the general election to be held on the Tuesday after the first Monday in November next, and in the city of Baltimore, on the fourth Wednesday of October next. Each of the said Judges shall hold his office for the term of fifteen years from the time of his election, and until his successor is elected and qualified, or until he shall have attained the age of seventy years, whichever may first happen, and be re-eligible thereto until he shall have attained the age of seventy years, and not after; but in case of any Judge, who shall attain the age of seventy years whilst in office, such Judge may be continued in office by the General Assembly for such further time as they may think fit, not to exceed the term for which he was elected, by a Resolution to be passed at the session next preceding his attaining said

Retiring Judges for inability. age. In case of the inability of any of said Judges to discharge his duties with efficiency, by reason of continued sickness, or of physical or mental infirmity, it shall be in the power of the General Assembly, two-thirds of the members of each House concurring, with the approval of the Governor, to retire said Judge from office.

Removal of Judges for incompetency, &c. SEC. 4. Any Judge shall be removed from office by the Governor, on conviction in a Court of Law, of incompetency, of wilful neglect of duty, misbehaviour in office, or any other crime, or on impeachment, according to this Constitution, or the Laws of the State; or on the address of the General Assembly, two-thirds of each House concurring in such address, and the accused having been notified of the charges against him, and having had opportunity of making his defence.

Governor to appoint in case of vacancy. SEC. 5. After the election for Judges, to be held as above mentioned, upon the expiration of the term, or in case of the death, resignation, removal, or other disqualification of any Judge, the Governor shall appoint a person duly qualified to fill said office, who shall hold the same until the next general election for members of the General Assembly, when a successor shall be elected, whose tenure of office shall be the same, as hereinbefore provided; but if the vacancy shall occur in the city of Baltimore, the time of election shall be the fourth Wednesday in October following.

SEC. 6. All Judges shall, by virtue of their offices, be Conservators of the Peace throughout the State; and no fees, or perquisites, commission, or reward of any kind, shall be allowed to any Judge in this State, besides his annual salary, for the discharge of any Judicial duty. *Judges to be Conservators of the Peace. No fees to Judges. 1 Md. 368; 8 Md. 227.*

SEC. 7. No Judge shall sit in any case wherein he may be interested, or where either of the parties may be connected with him, by affinity or consanguinity, within such degrees as now are, or may hereafter be prescribed by Law, or where he shall have been of counsel in the case. *Judges disqualified. 1852, c. 263; 22 Md. 458.*

SEC. 8. The parties to any cause may submit the same to the Court for determination, without the aid of a jury; and the Judge, or Judges of any Court of this State, except the Court of Appeals, shall order and direct the Record of proceedings in any suit, or action, issue, or petition, presentment, or indictment, pending in such Court, to be transmitted to some other Court, (and of a different Circuit, if the party applying shall so elect,) having jurisdiction in such cases, whenever any party to such cause, or the counsel of any party, shall make a suggestion, in writing, supported *Trial without Jury. Removal of cases. 6 H. & J. 270; 2 Md. 274; 5 Md. 370; 6 Md. 449; 7 Md. 135; 8 Md. 322; 11 Md. 362; 19 Md. 15; 20 Md. 18; 1852, c. 169, 315; 1854, c. 325*

5

by the affidavit of such party, or his counsel, or other proper evidence, that the party cannot have a fair or impartial trial in the Court, in which such suit, or action, issue, or petition, presentment, or indictment is pending, or when the Judges of said Court shall be disqualified, under the provisions of this Constitution, to sit in any such suit, action, issue or petition, presentment, or indictment; and the General Assembly shall make such modifications of existing Law as may be necessary to regulate and give force to this provision.

Officers of Court, how appointed.

SEC. 9. The Judge, or Judges of any Court, may appoint such officers. for their respective Courts as may be found necessary; and such officers of the Courts in the City of Baltimore shall be appointed by the Judges of the Supreme Bench of Baltimore City. It shall be the duty of the General Assembly to pre-

Compensation.

scribe, by Law, a fixed compensation for all such officers; and said Judge, or Judges shall,

Judges to investigate and report.

from time to time, investigate the expenses, costs and charges of their respective courts, with a view to a change or reduction thereof, and report the result of such investigation to the General Assembly for its action.

Clerks to keep Records.

SEC. 10. The Clerks of the several Courts, created, or continued by this Constitution, shall have charge and custody of the records and other papers, shall perform all the duties,

Fees.

and be allowed the fees, which appertain to their several offices, as the same now are, or may hereafter be regulated by Law. And the office and business of said Clerks, in all their departments, shall be subject to the visitorial power of the Judges of their respective Courts, ^{Power of} Judges. who shall exercise the same, from time to · time, so as to insure the faithful performance of the duties of said offices; and it shall be the duty of the Judges of said Courts respectively, to make, from time to time, such rules Rules for the Clerks. and regulations as may be necessary and proper for the government of said Clerks, and for the performance of the duties of their offices, which shall have the force of Law until repealed, or modified by the General Assembly.

SEC. 11. The election for Judges, herein- Election Returns. before provided, and all elections for Clerks, 1853, c. 134. Registers of Wills, and other officers, provided in this Constitution, except State's Attorneys, shall be certified, and the returns made, by the Clerks of the Circuit Courts of the Counties, and the Clerk of the Superior Court of Baltimore city, respectively, to the Governor, who shall issue commissions to the different persons for the offices to which they shall have been, respectively, elected; and in all such elections, the person having the greatest number of votes, shall be declared Plurality vote. to be elected.

SEC. 12. If in any case of election for Case of tie. Judges, Clerks of the Courts of Law, and Registers of Wills, the opposing candidates shall

have an equal number of votes, it shall be the
duty of the Governor to order a new election;
and in case of any contested election, the Governor shall send the returns to the House of
Delegates, which shall judge of the election
and qualification of the candidates at such
election; and if the judgment shall be against
the one who has been returned elected, or the
one who· has been commissioned by the Governor, the House of Delegates shall order a
new election within thirty days.

SEC. 13. All Public Commissions and Grants
shall run thus: " The State of Maryland, &c.,"
and shall be signed by the Governor, with the
Seal of the State annexed; all writs and process shall run in the same style, and be tested,
sealed and signed, as heretofore, or as may
hereafter be, provided by Law; and all indict-
ments shall conclude, " against the peace, government and dignity of the State."

PART II.   COURT OF APPEALS.

SEC. 14. The Court of Appeals shall be
composed of the Chief Judges of the first
seven of the several Judicial Circuits of the
State, and a Judge from the City of Baltimore
specially elected thereto, one of whom shall
be designated by the, Governor, by and with
the advice and consent of the Senate, as the
Chief Judge: and in all cases, until action

by the Senate can be had, the Judge so designated by the Governor, shall act as Chief Judge. The Judge of the Court of Appeals from the City of Baltimore shall be elected by the qualified voters of said City, at the election of Judges to be held therein, as hereinbefore provided; and in addition to his duties, as Judge of the Court of Appeals, shall perform such other duties as the General Assembly shall prescribe. The jurisdiction of said Court of Appeals shall be co-extensive with the limits of the State, and such as now is, or may hereafter be prescribed by Law. It shall hold its sessions in the city of Annapolis, on the first Monday in April, and the first Monday in October, of each and every year, or at such other times as the General Assembly may, by Law, direct. Its sessions shall continue not less than ten months in the year, if the business before it shall so require; and it shall be competent for the Judges, temporarily, to transfer their sittings elsewhere, upon sufficient cause.

SEC. 15. Four of said Judges shall constitute a quorum; no cause shall be decided without the concurrence of at least three; but the Judge who heard the cause below, shall not participate in the decision; in every case an opinion, in writing, shall be filed within three months after the argument, or submission of the cause; and the judgment of the Court shall be final and conclusive; and all

Hearing at first term.
20 Md. 58.

cases shall stand for hearing at the first term after the transmission of the Record.

Publishing Reports.
1852, c. 55, 351;
1854. res. 5.

SEC. 16. Provision shall be made by Law for publishing Reports of all causes, argued and determined in the Court of Appeals, which the Judges shall designate as proper for publication.

Clerk to be elected.

SEC. 17. There shall be a Clerk of the Court of Appeals, who shall be elected by the legal and qualified voters of the State, who shall hold his office for six years, and until his successor is duly qualified; he shall be subject to

Removal.

removal by the said Court for incompetency, neglect of duty, misdemeanor in office, or such other cause, or causes, as may be prescribed

Vacancy.

by Law ; and in case of a vacancy in the office of said Clerk, the Court of Appeals shall appoint a Clerk of said Court, who shall hold his office until the election and qualification of his successor, who shall be elected at the next general election for members of the General Assembly ; and the person, so elected, shall hold his office for the term of six years from the time of election.

Rules for Appeals.

SEC. 18. It shall be the duty of the Judges of the Court of Appeals, as soon after their election, under this Constitution, as practicable, to make and publish rules and regulations for the prosecution - of appeals to said appellate court, whereby they shall prescribe the periods within which appeals may be taken, what part or parts of the proceedings

in the Court below shall constitute the record The Record.
on appeal, and the manner in which such
appeals shall be brought to hearing or determination, and shall regulate, generally, the
practice of said Court of Appeals, so as to Practice.
prevent delays, and promote brevity in all
records and proceedings brought into said
Court, and to abolish and avoid all unnecessary costs and expenses in the prosecution of Costs.
appeals therein; and the said Judges shall
make such reductions in the fees and expenses Reduction of
Fees.
of the said Court, as they may deem advisable.
It shall also be the duty of said Judges of the
Court of Appeals, as soon after their election
as practicable, to devise, and promulgate by
rules, or orders, forms and modes of framing Rules in
Equity.
and filing bills, answers, and other proceedings and pleadings in Equity; and also forms
and modes of taking and obtaining evidence,
to be used in Equity cases; and to revise and
regulate, generally, the practice in the Courts
of Equity of this State, so as to prevent
delays, and to promote brevity and concise-
ness in all pleadings and proceedings therein,
and to abolish all unnecessary costs and expenses attending the same. And all rules
and regulations hereby directed to be made,
shall, when made, have the force of Law, until
rescinded, changed, or modified by the said
Judges, or the General Assembly.

PART III — CIRCUIT COURTS.

Eight Judicial Circuits.

SEC. 19. The State shall be divided into eight Judicial Circuits, in manner following, viz: the Counties of Worcester, Somerset and Dorchester, shall constitute the First Circuit; the Counties of Caroline, Talbot, Queen Anne's, Kent and Cecil, the Second; the Counties of Baltimore and Harford, the Third; the Counties of Allegany and Washington, the Fourth; the Counties of Carroll, Howard and Anne Arundel, the Fifth; the Counties of Montgomery and Frederick, the Sixth; the Counties of Prince George's, Charles, Calvert and St. Mary's, the Seventh; and Baltimore City, the Eighth.

A Court in each county.

SEC. 20. A Court shall be held in each County of the State, to be styled the Circuit Court for the County, in which it may be held. The said Circuit Courts shall have and exercise, in the respective Counties, all the power, authority and jurisdiction, original and appellate, which the present Circuit Courts of this State now have and exercise, or which may hereafter be prescribed by Law.

Jurisdiction. 1852, c. 16, 31, 75, 111, 136, 219, 336, 344; 1853, c. 181, 238, 406.

Chief Judge and two Associates.

SEC. 21. For each of the said Circuits (excepting the Eighth,) there shall be a Chief Judge, and two Associate Judges, to be styled Judges of the Circuit Court, to be elected or appointed, as herein provided. And no two of said Associate Judges shall, at the time of

·their election, or appointment, or during the
term, for which they may have been elected,
or appointed, reside in the same County. If   Residence.
two or more persons shall be candidates for
Associate Judge, in· the same County, that
one only ih said County shall be declared
elected, who has the highest number of votes
in the Circuit. In case any two candidates
for Associate Judge, residing in the same
County, shall have an.equal number of votes,   Case of tie.
greater than any other candidate for Associate
Judge, in the Circuit, it shall be the duty of
the Governor to order a new election for one
Associate Judge; but the person, residing in
any other County of the Circuit, and who has
the next highest number of votes shall be
declared elected. The said Judges shall hold
not less than two terms of the Circuit Court   Two Terms a
in each of the Counties, composing their ·re-   year.
spective Circuits, at such times as are now, or
may hereafter be prescribed, to which Jurors
shall be summoned; and in those Counties
where only two such Terms are held, two other
and intermediate Terms, to which Jurors shall   Intermediate
not be summoned; they may alter or fix the   Terms.
times for holding any, or all Terms until otherwise prescribed, and shall adopt Rules to the
end that all business not requiring the inter-
position of a Jury shall be, as far as practicable, disposed of at said intermediate Terms.
One Judge, in each of the above Circuits, shall   One Judge may
constitute a quorum for the transaction of any   sit.

business; and the said Judges, or any of them,

Special Terms. may hold Special Terms of their Courts, whenever, in their discretion, the business of the several Counties renders such Terms necessary.

Points reserved to be heard in banc. SEC. 22. Where any Term is held, or trial conducted by less than the whole number of said Circuit Judges, upon the decision, or determination of any point, or question, by the Court, it shall be competent to the party, against whom the ruling or decision is made, upon motion, to have the point, or question reserved for the consideration of the three Judges of the Circuit, who shall constitute a

Rules therefor. Court in *banc* for such purpose; and the motion for such reservation shall be entered of record, during the sitting, at which such decision may be made; and the several Circuit Courts shall regulate, by rules, the mode and manner of presenting such points, or questions to the Court in *banc,* and the decision of the said Court in *banc* shall be the effective decision in the premises, and conclusive, as against the party, at whose motion said points or questions were reserved; but such decision in

Right of Appeal not precluded. *banc* shall not preclude the right of Appeal, or writ of error to the adverse party, in those cases, civil or criminal, in which appeal, or writ of error to the Court of Ap-

Not to apply to Appeals from Justices of the Peace and certain criminal cases. peals may be allowed by Law. The right of having questions reserved shall not, however, apply to trials of Appeals from judgments of

Justices of the Peace, nor to criminal cases below the grade of felony, except when the punishment is confinement in the Penitentiary; and this Section shall be subject to such provisions as may hereafter be made by Law.

SEC. 23. The Judges of the respective Circuit Courts of this State, and of the Courts of Baltimore City, shall render their decisions, in all cases argued before them, or submitted for their judgment, within two months after the same shall have been so argued or submitted. *Opinions in two months.*

SEC. 24. The salary of each Chief Judge, and of the Judge of the Court of Appeals from the City of Baltimore shall be three thousand five hundred dollars, and of each Associate Judge of the Circuit Court, shall be two thousand eight hundred dollars per annum, payable quarterly, and shall not be diminished during his continuance in office. *Salaries not to be diminished.*

SEC. 25. There shall be a Clerk of the Circuit Court for each County, who shall be elected by a plurality of the qualified voters of said County, and shall hold his office for six years from the time of his election, and until his successor is elected and qualified, and be re-eligible, subject to be removed for wilful neglect of duty, or other misdemeanor in office, on conviction in a Court of Law. In case of a vacancy in the office of Clerk of a Circuit Court, the Judges of said Court shall *Clerks to be elected. 1853, c. 134; 11 Md. 296. Removal. 9 Md. 242; 1852, c. 173,308; 1853, c. 134, 409, 444; 1858, c. 363.*

Vacancy,
1 Md. 374; 11
Md. 101.

have power to fill such vacancy until the general election for Delegates to the General Assembly, to be held next thereafter, when a successor shall be elected for the term of six years.

SEC. 26. The said Clerks shall appoint, subject to the confirmation of the Judges of their respective Courts, as many deputies under them, as the said Judges shall deem necessary, to perform, together with themselves, the duties of the said office, who shall be removable by the said Judges for incompetency, or neglect of duty, and whose compensation shall be according to existing, or future provisions of the General Assembly.

PART IV—COURTS OF BALTIMORE CITY.

Six Courts.

SEC. 27. There shall be in the Eighth Judicial Circuit, six Courts, to be styled the Supreme Bench of Baltimore City, the Superior Court of Baltimore City, the Court of Common Pleas, the Baltimore City Court, the Circuit Court of Baltimore City, and the Criminal Court of Baltimore.

Jurisdiction.
7 Md. 135; 13 Md.
314; 1852, c. 159,
196, 227, 251, 312,
323; 1853, c. 86,
238, 451; 1858, c.
323; 5 Md. 337;
13 Md. 314; 14
Md. 173.

SEC. 28. The Superior Court of Baltimore City, the Court of Common Pleas, and the Baltimore City Court shall, each, have concurrent jurisdiction in all civil common Law cases, and, concurrently, all the jurisdiction which the Superior Court of Baltimore City and the Court of Common Pleas now have, except jurisdiction in Equity, and except in applications for the benefit of the Insolvent Laws of Maryland, and in cases of Appeal from judgments of Justices of the Peace in said City, whether civil or criminal, or arising under the ordinances of the Mayor and City Council of Baltimore, of all of which appeal cases the Baltimore City Court shall have exclusive jurisdiction; and the said Court of Common Pleas shall have exclusive jurisdiction in all applications for the benefit of the Insolvent Laws of Maryland, and the supervision and control of the Trustees thereof.

SEC. 29. The Circuit Court of Baltimore City shall have exclusive jurisdiction in Equity within the limits of said city, and all such jurisdiction as the present Circuit Court of Baltimore City has; provided, the said Court shall not have jurisdiction in applications for the writ of *habeas corpus* in cases of persons charged with criminal offences. *Jurisdiction of Circuit Court. 5 Md. 337; 19 Md. 606.*

SEC. 30. The Criminal Court of Baltimore shall have and exercise all the jurisdiction, now held and exercised by the Criminal Court of Baltimore, except in such Appeal Cases as are herein assigned to the Baltimore City Court. *Jurisdiction of Criminal Court. 1852, c. 344; 1853, c. 33.*

SEC. 31. There shall be elected by the legal and qualified voters of said City, at the election, hereinbefore provided for, one Chief Judge, and four Associate Judges, who, together, shall constitute the Supreme Bench of *Supreme Bench of Baltimore City.*

Baltimore City, and shall hold their offices for
the term of fifteen years, subject to the provisions of this Constitution with regard to the
election and qualifications of Judges, and their
removal from office, and shall exercise the
jurisdiction, hereinafter specified, and shall
each receive an annual salary of three thousand five hundred dollars, payable quarterly,
which shall not be diminished during their
term of office; but authority is hereby given
to the Mayor and City Council of Baltimore
to pay to each of the said Judges an annual
addition of five hundred dollars to their respective salaries; provided, that the same,
being once granted, shall not be diminished,
nor increased, during the continuance of said
Judges in office.

Sec. 32. It shall be the duty of the said
Supreme Bench of Baltimore City, as soon as
the Judges thereof shall be elected and duly
qualified, and from time to time, to provide
for the holding of each of the aforesaid Courts,
by the assignment of one, or more of their
number to each of the said Courts, who may
sit either, separately, or together, in the trial
of cases; and the said Supreme Bench of Baltimore City may, from time to time, change
the said assignment, as circumstances may require, and the public interest may demand;
and the Judge, or Judges, so assigned to the
said several Courts, shall, when holding the
same, have all the powers and exercise all the

Term 15 years.

Salary.

Assignment of Judges.

May be changed from time to time.

jurisdiction, which may belong to the Court _{Jurisdiction.}
so being held; and it shall also be the duty
of the said Supreme Bench of Baltimore City,
in case of the sickness, absence, or disability _{Sickness, absence, &c.}
of any Judge or Judges, assigned as afore-
said, to provide for the hearing of the cases,
or transaction of the business assigned to said
Judge, or Judges, as aforesaid, before some
one, or more of the Judges of said Court.

SEC. 33. The said Supreme Bench of Balti- _{General Terms.}
more City shall have power, and it shall be
its duty, to provide for the holding of as many
general Terms as the performance of its duties
may require, such general Terms to be held
by not less than three Judges; to make all
needful rules and regulations for the conduct _{Rules to be made.}
of business in each of the said Courts, during
the session thereof, and in vacation, or in
Chambers, before any of said Judges; and
shall also have jurisdiction to hear and de-
termine all motions for a new trial in cases _{Jurisdiction on motions.}
tried in any of said Courts, where such mo-
tions arise either, on questions of fact, or for
misdirection upon any matters of Law, and
all motions in arrest of judgment, or upon
any matters of Law determined by the said
Judge, or Judges, while holding said several
Courts; and the said Supreme Bench of Baltimore City shall make all needful rules and
regulations for the hearing before it of all
of said matters; and the same right of appeal _{Right of Appeal.}
to the Court of Appeals shall be allowed from

the determination of the said Court on such
matters, as would have been the right of the
parties if said matters had been decided by
the Court in which said cases were tried.

No appeal on
decisions on
appeal from
Justices of the
Peace.

SEC. 34. No appeal shall lie to the Supreme
Bench of Baltimore City from the decision of
the Judge, or Judges, holding the Baltimore
City Court, in case of appeal from a Justice
of the Peace; but the decision by said Judge,
or Judges, shall be final; and all writs and
other process issued out of either of said

Test of Writs.

Courts, requiring attestation, shall be attested
in the name of the Chief Judge of the said
Supreme Bench of Baltimore City.

Quorum three
Judges.

SEC. 35. Three of the Judges of said Supreme Bench of Baltimore City, shall constitute a quorum of said Court.

Cases pending
to be proceeded
with.

SEC. 36. All causes depending, at the adoption of this Constitution, in the Superior Court
of Baltimore City, the Court of Common Pleas,
the Criminal Court of Baltimore, and the Circuit Court of Baltimore City shall be proceeded in, and prosecuted to final judgment,
or decree, in the Courts, respectively, of the
same name established by this Constitution,
except cases belonging to that class, jurisdiction over which is by this Constitution trans-
ferred to the Baltimore City Court, all of
which shall, together with all cases now pending in the City Court of Baltimore, be proceeded in, and prosecuted to final judgment
in said Baltimore City Court.

SEC. 37. There shall be a Clerk of each of the said Courts of Baltimore City, except the Supreme Bench, who shall be elected by the legal and qualified voters of said City, at the election to be held in said city on the Tuesday next after the First Monday of November, in the year eighteen hundred and sixty-seven, and shall hold his office for six years from the time of his election, and until his successor is elected and qualified, and be re-eligible thereto, subject to be removed for wilful· neglect of duty, or other misdemeanor in office, on conviction in a Court of Law. The salary of each of the said Clerks shall be thirty-five hundred dollars a year, payable only out of the fees and receipts collected by the Clerks of said City, and they shall be entitled to no other perquisites, or compensation. In case of a vacancy in the office of Clerk of any of said Courts, the Judges of said Supreme Bench of Baltimore City shall have power to fill such vacancy until the general election of Delegates to the General Assembly, to be held next thereafter, when a Clerk of said Court shall be elected to serve for six years thereafter; and the provisions of this Article in relation to the appointment of Deputies by the Clerks of the Circuit Courts in the Counties shall apply to the Clerks of the Courts in Baltimore City.

Clerks to be elected by the people.

Term 6 years

Salaries $3,500.

Perquisites not allowed.

Vacancy.

SEC. 38. The Clerk of the Court of Common Pleas shall have authority to issue within said

Authority of Clerks of Common Pleas and Superior Court.

6

City, all marriage and other licenses required
by Law, subject to such provisions as are now,
or may be prescribed by Law. The Clerk of
the Superior Court of said City shall receive
and record all Deeds, Conveyances, and other
papers, which are, or may be required by
Law, to be recorded in said City. He shall
also have custody of all papers connected
with the proceedings on the Law, or Equity
side of Baltimore County Court, and of the
Dockets thereof, so far as the same have relation to the City of Baltimore, and shall also
discharge the duties of Clerk to the Supreme
Bench of Baltimore City, unless otherwise
provided by Law.

Another Court
in Baltimore
City.
1853, c. 122, 391.
1867, c. 401.

SEC. 39. The General Assembly shall, whenever it may think the same proper and expedient, provide, by Law, another Court for the
City of Baltimore, and prescribe its jurisdiction and powers; in which case there shall be
elected by the voters of said City, qualified
under this Constitution, another Judge of the
Supreme Bench of Baltimore City, who shall
be subject to the same constitutional provisions, hold his office for the same term of
years, receive the same compensation, and
have the same powers, as are herein provided
for the Judges of said Supreme Bench of Baltimore City; and all of the provisions of this
Constitution relating to the assignment of
Judges to the Courts, now existing in said
City, and for the dispatch of business therein,

shall apply to the Court, for whose creation provision is made by this Section. And the General Assembly may reapportion, change, Reapportionment of Jurisdiction of Baltimore Courts. or enlarge the jurisdiction of the several Courts in Baltimore City. Until otherwise provided by Law, the Clerk of the Superior Court of Baltimore City, of the Court of Common Pleas, of the Circuit Court of Baltimore City, of the Baltimore City Court, and of the Criminal Court of Baltimore, shall each give Bond in such penalty as is now prescribed, by Clerks' Bonds. Law, to be given by the Clerks of the Courts, bearing the same names, under the present Constitution.

PART V—ORPHANS' COURTS.

SEC. 40. The qualified voters of the City of Three Judges. Baltimore, and of the several Counties, shall on the Tuesday next after the first Monday in November next, and on the same day in every fourth year thereafter, elect three men to be Term four years. Judges of the Orphans' Courts of said City 1852, c. 20, 48, 62, 73, 139, 247, 200, and Counties, respectively, who shall be citi- 341. 1853, c. 81, 147, 271, 333, 385. zens of the State, and residents for the twelve months preceding, in the City, or County, for which they may be elected. They shall have all the powers now vested in the Orphans' Jurisdiction. Courts of the State, subject to such changes as the Legislature may prescribe. Each of said Judges shall be paid a per diem for the Per Diem.

time they are actually in session, to be regulated by Law, and to be paid by the said City, or Counties respectively. In case of a

Vacancy. vacancy in the office of Judge of the Orphans' Court, the Governor shall appoint, subject to confirmation, or rejection by the Senate, some suitable person to fill the same for the residue of the term.

Register of Wills.
14 Md. 40.
SEC. 41. There shall be a Register of Wills in each county of the State, and the city of Baltimore, to be elected by the legal and qualified voters of said counties and city, respectively, who shall hold his office for six

Term six years. years from the time of his election, and until his successor is elected and qualified; he shall be re-eligible, and subject at all times to removal for wilful neglect of duty, or misdemeanor in office in the same manner that the Clerks of the Courts are removable. In the

Vacancy. event of any vacancy in the office of Register of Wills, said vacancy shall be filled by the Judges of the Orphans' Court, in which such vacancy occurs, until the next general election for Delegates to the General Assembly, when a Register shall be elected to serve for six years thereafter.

PART VI—JUSTICES OF THE PEACE.

Governor to appoint Justices.
SEC. 42. The Governor, by and with the advice and consent of the Senate, shall ap-

point such number of Justices of the Peace,
and the County Commissioners of the several
counties, and the Mayor and City Council of
Baltimore, respectively, shall appoint such
number of Constables, for the several Elec- County Commissioners and
tion Districts of the Counties, and Wards of point Consta-
the City of Baltimore, as are now, or may 1852, c. 274; 1853, c. 102; 1854, c.
hereafter be prescribed by Law; and Justices 302; 14 Md. 215.
of the Peace and Constables, so appointed,
shall be subject to removal by the Judge, or Removal.
Judges, having criminal jurisdiction in the
county, or city, for incompetency, wilful neglect of duty, or misdemeanor in office, on
conviction in a Court of Law.· The Justices
of the Peace and Constables, so appointed,
and commissioned, shall be Conservators of
the Peace, shall hold their office for two years, Term two years.
and shall have such jurisdiction, duties and Jurisdiction.
1852, c. 176, 239;
compensation, subject to such right of appeal, 1853, c. 201; 1854, c. 225, 236; 5 Md.
in all cases, from the judgment of Justices of 337.
the Peace, as hath been heretofore exercised,
or shall be hereafter prescribed by Law.

SEC. 43. In the event of a vacancy in the Vacancies.
14 Md. 215; 15
office of a Justice of the Peace, the Governor Md. 376; 1800, c. 7.
shall appoint a person to serve, as Justice of
the Peace, for the residue of the term; and in
case of a vacancy in the office of Constable,
the County Commissioners of the county in
which the vacancy occurs, or the Mayor and
City Council of Baltimore, as the case may
be, shall appoint a person to serve as Constable for the residue of the term.

PART VII — SHERIFFS.

Election.

SEC. 44. There shall be elected in each county, and in the City of Baltimore, in every second year, one person, resident in

Qualification.
2 G. 487.

said county or city, above the age of twenty-five years, and at least five years preceding his election, a citizen of this State, to the office of Sheriff. He shall hold his office for

Term two
years.

two years, and until his successor is duly elected and qualified; shall be ineligible for

Bond.

two years thereafter, shall give such bond, exercise such powers, and perform such duties as now are, or may hereafter be fixed by Law.

Vacancy.

In case of a vacancy by death, resignation, refusal to serve, or neglect to qualify, or give bond, or by disqualification, or removal from the county, or city, the Governor shall appoint a person to be Sheriff for the remainder of the official term.

Coroners, &c.

SEC. 45. Coroners, Elisors, and Notaries Public may be appointed for each county, and the city of Baltimore, in the manner, for the purpose, and with the powers now fixed, or which may hereafter be prescribed by Law.

ARTICLE V.

Attorney General and State's Attorneys.

Attorney General.

Section 1. There shall be an Attorney- Election. General elected by the qualified voters of the State, on general ticket, on the Tuesday next after the first Monday in the month of November, Eighteen hundred and sixty-seven, and on the same day, in every fourth year thereafter, who shall hold his office for four Term four years. years from the time of his election and qualification, and until his successor is elected and qualified, and shall be re-eligible thereto, and Removal. shall be subject to removal for incompetency, wilful neglect of duty, or misdemeanor in office, on conviction in a Court of Law.

Sec. 2. All elections for Attorney-General Returns to be made to Governor. shall be certified to, and returns made thereof by the Clerks of the Circuit Courts of the several counties, and the Clerk of the Superior Court of Baltimore City, to the Governor of the State, whose duty it shall be to decide on the election and qualification of the person returned; and in case of a tie between two or more Case of tie. persons, to designate which of said persons shall qualify as Attorney General, and to administer the oath of office to the person elected.

Sec. 3. It shall be the duty of the Attorney Duties General to prosecute and defend on the part of the State, all cases, which at the time of his appointment and qualification, and which thereafter may be depending in the Court of Appeals, or in the Supreme Court of the United States, by or against the State, or wherein the State may be interested; and he shall give his opinion in writing. whenever required by the General Assembly, or either Branch thereof, the Governor, the Comptroller, the Treasurer, or any State's Attorney, on any legal matter, or subject depending before them, or either of them; and when required by the Governor, or the General Assembly, he shall aid any State's Attorney in prosecuting any suit or action brought by the State in any Court of this State; and he shall commence and prosecute, or defend, any suit or action in any of said Courts, on the part of the State, which the General Assembly, or the Governor, acting according to Law, shall direct to be commenced, prosecuted or defended; and he shall receive for his services an annual salary of Three Thousand dollars; but he shall not be entitled to receive any fees, perquisites, or rewards, whatever, in addition to the salary aforesaid, for the performance of any official duty; nor have power to appoint any agent, representative, or deputy, under any circumstances, whatever; nor shall the Governor employ any additional counsel in any case, whatever, unless authorized by the General Assembly.

Opinions to be given when required.

Prosecute suits.

Salary, $3,000.

Perquisites not allowed.

Other Counsel not to be employed.

SEC. 4. No person shall be eligible to the Qualifications. office of Attorney General, who is not a citizen of this State, and a qualified voter therein, and has not resided and practiced Law in this State for at least ten years.

SEC. 5. In case of vacancy in the office Vacancy. of Attorney General, occasioned by death, resignation, removal from the State, or from office, or other disqualification, the said vacancy shall be filled by the Governor, for the residue of the term thus made vacant.

SEC. 6. It shall be the duty of the Clerk of Attorney General to be notified the Court of Appeals and of the Commis- of State cases. sioner of the Land Office, respectively, whenever a case shall be brought into said Court, or office, in which the State is a party, or has interest, immediately to notify the Attorney-General thereof.

THE STATE'S ATTORNEYS.

SEC. 7 There shall be an Attorney for the Election. State in each county, and the city of Baltimore, to be styled "The State's Attorney," who shall be elected by the voters thereof, respectively, on the Tuesday next after the first Monday in November in the year eighteen hundred and sixty-seven, and on the same day every fourth year thereafter; and shall hold his office for four years from the Term four years. first Monday in January next ensuing his election, and until his successor shall be elected and qualified; and shall be re-eligible

Removal. thereto, and be subject to removal therefrom, for incompetency, wilful neglect of duty, or misdemeanor in office, on conviction in a Court of Law, or by a vote of two-thirds of the Senate, on the recommendation of the Attorney General.

Returns to be made to Criminal Judges. Sec. 8. All elections for the State's Attorney shall be certified to, and Returns made thereof, by the Clerks of the said counties and city, to the Judges thereof, having criminal jurisdiction, respectively, whose duty it shall be to decide upon the elections and qualifications of the ·Persons returned; and, in case

Case of tie. of a tie between two or more Persons, to designate which of said Persons shall qualify as State's Attorney, and to administer the oaths of office to the Person elected.

Fees. Sec. 9. The State's Attorney shall perform such duties and receive such fees and commissions as are now, or may hereafter be, prescribed by law, and if any State's Attorney shall receive any other fee or reward, than such as is, or may be allowed by Law, he shall, on conviction thereof, be removed from

Deputy in Baltimore City. office; *provided*, that the State's Attorney for Baltimore City shall have power to appoint one Deputy, at a salary of not more than Fifteen Hundred dollars per annum, to be paid by the State's Attorney out of the fees of his office, as has heretofore been practiced.

SEC. 10. No person shall be eligible to the Qualifications. office of State's Attorney, who has not been admitted to practice Law in this State, and who has not resided, for at least two years, in the county, or city, in which he may be elected.

SEC. 11. In case of vacancy in the office of Vacancy. State's Attorney, or, of his removal from the county, or city, in which he shall have been elected, or, on his conviction, as herein specified, the said vacancy shall be filled by the Judge of the county, or city, respectively, having criminal jurisdiction, in which said vacancy shall occur, for the residue of the term thus made vacant.

SEC. 12. The State's Attorney, in each Collect money for the State. county, and the city of Baltimore, shall have authority to collect, and give receipt, in the name of the State, for such sums of money as may be collected by him, and forthwith make return of, and pay over the same, to the proper accounting officer. And the State's Attorney of each county, and the city of Baltimore, before he shall enter on the discharge of his duties, shall execute a Bond to the State of Maryland, for the faithful performance of his duties, in the penalty of ten thousand dollars, Bond $10,000. with two or more sureties, to be approved by the Judge of the Court, having criminal jurisdiction, in said counties or city.

ARTICLE VI.

TREASURY DEPARTMENT.

Comptroller and Treasurer.

SECTION 1. There shall be a Treasury Department, consisting of a Comptroller, chosen by the qualified electors of the State, at each regular election of members of the House of Delegates, who shall receive an annual

Salaries $2,500 each.

4 Md. 189; 1853, c. 403; 1852, c. 12.

salary of Two Thousand Five Hundred dollars; and a Treasurer to be appointed by the two Houses of the Legislature, at each regular session thereof, on joint ballot, who shall receive an annual salary of Two Thousand Five Hundred dollars; and the terms of office of the said Comptroller and Treasurer shall

Terms two years.

be for two years, and until their successors shall qualify; and neither of the said officers

Perquisites not allowed.

shall be allowed, or receive any fees, commissions or perquisites of any kind, in addition to his salary, for the performance of any duty

Vacancy.

or services whatsoever. In case of a vacancy in either of the offices, by death, or otherwise, the Governor, by and with the advice and consent of the Senate, shall fill such vacancy, by appointment to continue until another election, or a choice by the Legislature, as the case may be, and until the qualification of the successor. The Comptroller and the

Office.

Treasurer shall keep their offices at the seat of Government, and shall take such oath, and

enter into such bonds for the faithful dis- Bond.
charge of their duties, as are now, or may
hereafter be, prescribed by Law.

SEC. 2. The Comptroller shall have the Comptroller's duties.
general superintendence of the fiscal affairs of
the State; he shall digest and prepare plans
for the improvement and management of the
Revenue, and for the support of the Public
Credit; prepare and report estimates of the
Revenue and Expenditures of the State; su- Revenue plans.
perintend and enforce the prompt collection Collection of Taxes.
of all Taxes and Revenue; adjust and settle, Delinquent Collectors.
on terms, prescribed by Law, with delinquent
Collectors and Receivers of taxes and State
revenue; preserve all Public Accounts; de-
cide on the forms of keeping and stating Ac- Forms of Accounts.
counts; grant, under regulations, prescribed
by Law, all warrants for money to be paid Warrants for money.
out of the Treasury, in pursuance of appro- 1841, March Session, c. 23; 1852,
priations by Law; and countersign all checks c. 56, 65; 1853, c. 82, 86; 14 Md.
drawn by the Treasurer upon any Bank or 369.
Banks, in which the moneys of the State may,
from time to time, be deposited; prescribe
the formalities of the transfer of stock, or
other evidence of the State Debt, and countersign the same, without which, such Evidence shall not be valid; he shall make to
the General Assembly full Reports of all his Reports to Legislature.
proceedings, and of the state of the Treasury
Department, within ten days after the commencement of each Session; and perform such
other duties as shall be prescribed by Law.

Sec. 3. The Treasurer shall receive the moneys of the State, and, until otherwise prescribed by Law, deposit them, as soon as received, to the credit of the State, in such Bank, or Banks, as he may, from time to time, with the approval of the Governor, select, (the said Bank or Banks giving security, satisfactory to the Governor, for the safe keeping and forthcoming, when required, of said Deposits,) and shall disburse the same for the purposes of the State, according to Law, upon warrants drawn by the Comptroller, and on checks, countersigned by him, and not otherwise; he shall take receipts for all moneys paid by him; and receipts for moneys received by him shall be endorsed upon warrants, signed by the Comptroller; without which warrants, so signed, no acknowledgment of money received into the Treasury shall be valid; and upon warrants, issued by the Comptroller, he shall make arrangements for the payment of the interest of the Public Debt, and for the purchase thereof on account of the Sinking Fund. Every Bond, Certificate, or other Evidence of the debt of the State, shall be signed by the Treasurer, and countersigned by the Comptroller; and no new Certificate, or other Evidence intended to replace another, shall be issued until the old one shall be delivered to the Treasurer, and authority executed in due form for the transfer of the same filed in his office, and the

transfer accordingly made on the books thereof, and the certificate or other evidence can-
celled; but the Legislature may make provi-
sions for the loss of certificates, or other evi- Loss of Bonds.
dences of the debt; and may prescribe by
Law, the manner in which the Treasurer shall
receive and keep the moneys of the State.

SEC. 4. The Treasurer shall render his Treasurer
to render
Accounts, quarterly, to the Comptroller; and accounts to
Comptroller,
shall publish, monthly, in such newspapers as and to Legislature.
the Governor may direct, an abstract thereof,
showing the amount of cash on hand, and the
place, or places of deposit thereof; and on
the third day of each regular session of the
Legislature, he shall submit to the Senate and
House of Delegates fair and accurate copies
of all Accounts by him, from time to time,
rendered and settled with the Comptroller.
He shall, at all times, submit to the Comptroller the inspection of the money in his hands,
and perform all other duties that shall be
prescribed by Law.

SEC. 5. The Comptroller shall qualify, and When Comptroller and
enter on the duties of his office, on the third Treasurer
to qualify.
Monday of January next succeeding the time
of his election, or as soon thereafter as practicable. And the Treasurer shall qualify within
one month after his appointment by the Legislature.

SEC. 6. Whenever during the recess of the Governor may
remove Comp-
Legislature charges shall be preferred to the troller and
Treasurer.
Governor against the Comptroller or Trea-

surer, for incompetency, malfeasance in office, wilful neglect of duty, or misappropriation of the funds of the State, it shall be the duty of the Governor forthwith to notify the party so charged, and fix a day for a hearing of said charges; and if, from the evidence taken, under oath, on said hearing before the Governor, the said allegations shall be sustained, it shall be the duty of the Governor to remove said offending officer, and appoint another in his place, who shall hold the office for the unexpired term of the officer so removed.

ARTICLE VII.

SUNDRY OFFICERS.

County Commissioners.
6 Md. 468; 20
Md. 459; 1853, c.
173. 220, 239, 372;
1865, c. 85; 1866,
c. 134.

SECTION 1. County Commissioners shall be elected on general ticket of each County, by the qualified voters of the several Counties of this State, on the Tuesday next after the first Monday in the month of November, eighteen hundred and sixty seven, and on the same day in every second year thereafter. Their number in each County, their compensation, powers and duties, shall be such as are now, or may be hereafter prescribed by Law.

Surveyor.
1852, c. 69.

SEC. 2. The qualified voters of each County, and of the City of Baltimore, shall, on the

Tuesday next after the first Monday in the
month of November, in the year eighteen
hundred and sixty-seven, and on the same
day in every second year thereafter, elect a
Surveyor for each County and the City of
Baltimore, respectively, whose term of office
shall commence on the first Monday of January next ensuing their election; and whose
duties and compensation shall be the same
as are now, or may hereafter be prescribed by
Law. And any vacancy in the office of Sur- Vacancy.
veyor, shall be filled by the Commissioners of
the Counties, or by the Mayor and City Council of Baltimore, respectively, for the residue
of the term.

SEC. 3. The State Librarian shall be ap- State Librarian.
pointed by the Governor, by and with the 5 Md. 423; 1856,
c. 314.
advice and consent of the Senate and shall
hold his office during the term of the Governor, by whom he shall have been appointed,
and until his successor shall be appointed and
qualified. His salary shall be Fifteen hun- Salary $1,500.
dred dollars a year; and he shall perform such
duties as are now, or may hereafter be prescribed by Law; and no appropriation shall
be made by Law, to pay for any Clerk, or
assistant to the Librarian: And it shall be
the duty of the Legislature, at its first Session after the adoption of this Constitution,
to pass a Law regulating the mode and
manner in which the Books in the Library
shall be kept and accounted for by the Li-

7 *

brarian, and requiring the Librarian to give

Bond. a Bond, in such penalty as the Legislature may prescribe, for the proper discharge of his duties.

Commissioner of Land Office.
1852, c. 861; 1853, c. 415

SEC. 4. There shall be a Commissioner of the Land Office, who shall be appointed by the Governor, by and with the advice and consent of the Senate, who shall hold his office during the term of the Governor, by whom he shall have been appointed, and until his successor shall be appointed and **Duties.** qualified. He shall perform such duties as are now required of the Commissioner of the Land Office, or such as may hereafter be prescribed by Law, and shall also be the Keeper of the Chancery Records. He shall receive a **Salary $1,500** salary of One Thousand five hundred dollars per annum, to be paid out of the Treasury, and shall charge such fees as are now, or may be hereafter fixed by Law. He shall make a **Report his fees.** semi-annual report of all the fees of his office, both as Commissioner of the Land Office, and as Keeper of the Chancery Records, to the Comptroller of the Treasury, and shall pay the same semi-annually into the Treasury.

Collect all State Papers

SEC. 5. The Commissioner of the Land Office shall also, without additional compensation, collect, arrange, classify, have charge of, and safely keep all Papers, Records, Relics, and other Memorials connected with the Early History of Maryland, not belonging to any other office.

SEC. 6. The qualified voters of Worcester County shall, on the Tuesday next after the first Monday in the month of November in the year Eighteen Hundred and Sixty-seven, and every two years thereafter, elect a Wreck Master for said County, whose duties and compensation shall be the same as are now, or may be hereafter, prescribed by Law; the term of office of said Wreck Master shall commence on the first Monday of January, next succeeding his election, and a vacancy in said office shall be filled by the County Commissioners of said County for the residue of the term.

Wreck Master.

Vacancy.

ARTICLE VIII.

EDUCATION.

SECTION 1. The General Assembly, at its First Session after the adoption of this Constitution, shall by Law establish throughout the State a thorough and efficient System of Free Public Schools; and shall provide by taxation, or otherwise, for their maintenance.

System of Free Schools. 1865, c. 1, 160; 1867, c. 123.

Taxation. 1865, res. 11.

SEC. 2. The System of Public Schools, as now constituted, shall remain in force until the end of the said First Session of the General Assembly, and shall then expire; except

Present System to expire.

so far as adopted, or continued, by the General Assembly.

School Fund inviolate.   SEC. 3. The School Fund of the State shall be kept inviolate, and appropriated only to the purposes of Education.

ARTICLE IX.

MILITIA AND MILITARY AFFAIRS.

Organization and equipment.   SECTION 1. The General Assembly shall make, from time to time, such provision for organizing, equipping and disciplining the Militia, as the exigency may require, and *Volunteers.* pass such Laws to promote Volunteer Militia Organizations as may afford them effectual encouragement.

Adjutant General.

2 Md. 341.   SEC. 2. There shall be an Adjutant General, appointed by the Governor, by and with the advice and consent of the Senate. He shall hold his office until the appointment and qualification of his successor, or until removed in pursuance of the sentence of a Court *Court Martial.* Martial. He shall perform such duties, and receive such compensation, or emoluments, as are now, or may be prescribed by Law. He *Duties.* shall discharge the duties of his office at the seat of Government, unless absent, under orders, on duty; and no other officer of the

General Staff of the Militia shall receive salary or pay, except when on service, and mustered in with troops. Salary.

'SEC. 3. The existing Militia Law of the State shall expire at the end of the next Session of the General Assembly, except so far as it may be re-enacted, subject to the provisions of this Article. Existing Law to expire.
1853, c. 343.

ARTICLE X.

LABOR AND AGRICULTURE.

SECTION 1. There shall be a Superintendent of Labor and Agriculture, elected by the qualified voters of this State at the first general election for Delegates to the General Assembly after the adoption of this Constitution, who shall hold his office for the term of four years, and until the election and qualification of his successor. Superintendent. Term four years.

SEC. 2. His qualifications shall be the same as those prescribed for the Comptroller; he shall qualify and enter upon the duties of his office on the second Monday of January next, succeeding the time of his election; and a vacancy in the office shall be filled by the Governor for the residue of the term. Qualifications. Enter office. Vacancy.

SEC. 3. He shall perform such of the duties now devolved by Law upon the Commissioner of Immigration, and the Immigration Agent, as will promote the object, for which those officers were appointed, and such other duties as may be assigned to him by the General Assembly, and shall receive a salary of Twenty-five Hundred dollars a year; and after his election and qualification, the offices before mentioned shall cease.

SEC. 4. He shall supervise all the State Inspectors of agricultural products and fertilizers; and from time to time, shall carefully examine and audit their accounts, and prescribe regulations, not inconsistent with Law, tending to secure economy and efficiency in the business of their offices. He shall have the supervision of the Tobacco ·Warehouses, and all other buildings used for inspection and storage purposes by the State; and may, at the discretion of the Legislature, have the supervision of all public buildings, now belonging to, or which may hereafter be erected by the State. He shall frequently inspect such buildings as are committed to his charge, and examine all accounts for labor and materials required for their construction, or repairs.

SEC. 5. He shall inquire into the undeveloped resources of wealth of the State of Maryland more especially concerning those within the limits of the Chesapeake Bay and

its tributaries, which belong to the State, and
suggest such plans as may be calculated to
render them available as sources of revenue. Revenue.

SEC. 6. He shall make detailed reports to Reports.
every General Assembly within the first week
of its session, in reference to each of the subjects committed to his charge, and he shall
also report to the Governor, in the recess of
the Legislature, all abuses, or irregularities,
which he may find to exist in any Department
of public affairs, with which his office is connected.

SEC. 7. The office hereby established shall Office to Expire.
continue for four years from the date of the
qualification of the first incumbent thereof;
and shall then expire, unless continued by
the General Assembly.

ARTICLE XI.

CITY OF BALTIMORE.

SECTION 1. The Inhabitants of the City of Mayor.
Baltimore, qualified by Law to vote in said
city for members of the House of Delegates,
shall on the fourth Wednesday of October,
eighteen hundred and sixty-seven, and on the
same day in every fourth year thereafter, elect
a person to be Mayor of the City of Baltimore,

who shall have such qualifications, receive such compensation, discharge such duties, and have such powers as are now, or may hereafter be prescribed by Law; and the term of whose office shall commence on the first Monday of November succeeding his election, and

Term four years.

shall continue for four years, and until his successor shall have qualified; and he shall

Ineligible.

be ineligible for the term next succeeding that for which he was elected.

City Council.

Two Branches.

SEC. 2. The City Council of Baltimore shall consist of Two Branches, one of which shall be called the First Branch, and the other the Second Branch; and each shall consist of such number of members, having such qualification, receiving such compensation, performing such duties, possessing such powers, holding such terms of office, and elected in such manner, as are now, or may hereafter be prescribed by Law.

Time of Elections.

SEC. 3. An election for members of the First and Second Branch of the City Council of Baltimore shall be held in the City of Baltimore on the fourth Wednesday of October, eighteen hundred and sixty-seven; and for members of the First Branch on the same day in every year thereafter; and for members of the Second Branch on the same day in every second year thereafter; and the qualification for electors of the members of the City Council shall be the same as those prescribed for the electors of Mayor.

SEC. 4. The regular sessions of the City *Annual Sessions to continue ninety days.* Council of Baltimore, (which shall be annual,) shall commence on the third Monday of January of each year, and shall not continue more than ninety days, exclusive of Sundays; but the Mayor may convene the City Council in extra session whenever, and *Extra Sessions twenty days.* as often as it may appear to him that the public good may require; but no called, or extra session shall last longer than twenty days, exclusive of Sundays.

SEC. 5. No person, elected and qualified as *Members not to hold any other office.* Mayor, or as a member of the City Council, shall, during the term for which he was elected, hold any other office of profit or trust, created, or to be created, by the Mayor and City Council of Baltimore, or by any Law relating to the Corporation of Baltimore, or hold any employment, or position, the compensation of which shall be paid, directly or indirectly, out of the City Treasury; nor *Nor be interested in contracts.* shall any such person be interested, directly or indirectly, in any contract, to which the City is a party; nor shall it be lawful for any person, holding any office, under the City, to be interested, while holding such office, in any contract, to which the City is a party.

SEC. 6. The Mayor shall, on conviction in a *Mayor may be removed.* Court of Law, of wilful neglect of duty, or misbehavior in office, be removed from office by the Governor of the State, and a successor

shall thereafter be elected, as in a case of
vacancy.

No Debt to be
created or
credit given
without autho-
rity of Legisla-
ture and appro-
val of voters.

SEC. 7. From and after the adoption of this
Constitution, no debt (except as hereinafter
excepted,) shall be created by the Mayor
and City Council of Baltimore; nor shall the
credit of the Mayor and City Council of Baltimore be given, or loaned to, or in aid of any
individual, association, or corporation; nor
shall the Mayor and City Council of Baltimore have the power to involve the City of
Baltimore in the construction of Works of
Internal Improvement, nor in granting any
aid thereto, which shall involve the faith and
credit of the City, nor make any appropriation therefor, unless such debt, or credit be
authorized by an Act of the General Assembly of Maryland, and by an Ordinance of the
Mayor and City Council of Baltimore, submitted to the legal voters of the City of Baltimore at such time and place as may be
fixed by said Ordinance, and approved by a
majority of the votes cast at such time and
place; but the Mayor and City Council may,
temporarily, borrow any amount of money to
meet any deficiency in the City Treasury, or
to provide for any emergency arising from

Police.

the necessity of maintaining the Police, or
preserving the safety and sanitary condition
of the City, and may make due and proper
arrangements and agreements for the remo-

Extension of
Debts.

val and extension, in whole or in part, of any

and all debts and obligations, created according to Law before the adoption of this Constitution.

SEC. 8. All Laws and Ordinances, now in force, applicable to the City of Baltimore, not inconsistent with this Article, shall be, and they are hereby continued until changed in due course of Law. *Laws now in force continued.*

SEC. 9. The General Assembly may make such changes in this Article, except in Section seventh thereof, as it may deem best; and this Article shall not be so construed, or taken as to make the political Corporation of Baltimore independent, of, or free from the control, which the General Assembly of Maryland has over all such Corporations in this State. *General Assembly may make changes.* *City Corporation under its control.*

ARTICLE XII.

PUBLIC WORKS.

SECTION 1. The Governor, the Comptroller of the Treasury, and the Treasurer, shall constitute the Board of Public Works in this State. They shall keep a journal of their proceedings, and shall hold regular sessions in the City of Annapolis, on the first Wednesday in January, April, July and October, in each year, and oftener, if necessary; at *Board constituted of Governor, Comptroller and Treasurer.* *Regular Sessions.*

Powers. which sessions they shall hear and determine such· matters as affect the Public Works of the State, and as the General Assembly may confer upon them the power to decide.

Vote Stock. SEC. 2. They shall exercise a diligent and faithful supervision of all Public Works in which the State may ·be interested as Stockholder or Creditor, and shall represent, and vote the stock of the State of Maryland, in all meetings of the stockholders of the Chesa- *Appoint Directors.* peake and Ohio Canal; and shall appoint the Directors in every Railroad and Canal Company, in which the State. has the legal power to appoint Directors, which said Directors shall represent the State in all meetings of the Stockholders of the respective Companies, for which they are appointed or elected. And *Chesapeake and Ohio Canal Co.* the President and Directors of the said Chesapeake and Ohio Canal Company shall so regulate the tolls of said Company, from time to time, as to produce the largest amount of revenue, and to avoid the injurious effects to said Company of rival competition by other Internal Improvement Companies. They shall require the Directors of all said Public Works to guard the public interest, and prevent the *Rates of toll.* establishment of tolls which shall discriminate against the interest of the citizens or products of this State, and from time to time, and as often as there shall. be any change in the rates of toll on any of the said Works, to *Reports. 1852, c. 122.* furnish the said Board of Public Works a schedule of such modified rates of toll, and so adjust them as to promote the agricultural interests of the State; they shall report to the General Assembly at each regular session, and recommend such legislation as they may deem necessary and requisite to promote or protect the interests of the State in the said Public Works; they shall perform such other duties as may be hereafter prescribed by Law; and a majority of them shall be competent to act. The Governor, Comptroller and Treasurer shall receive no additional salary for services rendered by them as members of the Board of Public Works. The provisions of the Act of the General Assembly of Maryland of the year 1867, chapter 359, are hereby declared null and void.

Act of 1867, c. 359, declared void.

SEC. 3. The Board of Public Works is hereby authorized to exchange the State's interest as Stockholder and Creditor in the Baltimore and Ohio Railroad Company for an equal amount of the bonds or registered debt now owing by the State, to the extent only of all the preferred stock of the State on which the State is entitled to only six per cent. interest, provided such exchange shall not be made at less than par, nor less than the market value of said stock and the said Board is authorized subject to such regulations and conditions as the General Assembly may from time to time prescribe, to sell the State's interest in the other Works of Inter-

Baltimore and Ohio Rail Road Co. exchange of State's interest for Bonds.

Board may sell State's interest in other Works.

nal Improvement, whether as a Stockholder
or a Creditor, and also the State's interest in
any banking corporation, receiving in payment the bonds and registered debt now
owing by the State, equal in amount to the
price obtained for the State's said interest;
provided, that the interest of the State in the
Washington Branch of the Baltimore and
Ohio Rail Road be reserved and excepted
from sale; and provided further, that no sale
or contract of sale of the State's interest in the
Chesapeake and Ohio Canal, the Chesapeake
and Delaware Canal, and the Susquehanna
and Tide-water Canal Companies shall go
into effect until the same shall be ratified by
the ensuing General Assembly.

Banks.

Washington
Branch.

Ratification
by General
Assembly.

ARTICLE XIII.

NEW COUNTIES.

County seats
and lines.
1 Md.139; 15 Md.
549.

Consent of
Voters.

SECTION 1. The General Assembly may
provide, by Law, for organizing new Counties, locating and removing county seats, and
changing county lines; but no new county
shall be organized without the consent of the
majority of the legal voters residing within
the limits proposed to be formed into said
new county; and whenever a new county

shall be proposed to be formed out of portions
of two or more Counties, the consent of a majority of the legal voters of such part of each
of said counties, respectively, shall be required; nor shall the lines of any county be
changed without the consent of a majority of
the legal voters, residing within the district,
which, under said proposed change, would
form a part of a county different from that to
which it belonged prior to said change; and
no new county shall contain less than four
hundred square miles, nor less than ten thousand white Inhabitants; nor shall any change
be made in the limits of any county, whereby the population of said county would be
reduced to less than ten thousand white
Inhabitants, or its territory reduced to less
than four hundred square miles.

No new county without 10,000 white inhabitants and 400 square miles.

SEC. 2. At the election to be held for the
adoption, or rejection of this Constitution,
in each Election District, in those parts of
Worcester and Somerset Counties, comprised
within the following limits, viz: Beginning
at the point, where Mason and Dixon's line
crosses the channel of Pocomoke River, thence
following said line to the channel of the Nanticoke River, thence with the channel of said
river to Tangier Sound, or the intersection of
Nanticoke and Wicomico Rivers, thence up
the channel of the Wicomico River to the
mouth of Wicomico Creek, thence with the
•channel of said creek and Passerdyke Creek

Wicomico county.

Boundaries.

to Dashield's, or Disharoon's Mills, thence
with the mill-pond of said mills and Branch
following the middle prong of said Branch, to
Meadow Bridge, on the road, dividing the
Counties of Somerset and Worcester, near
the southwest corner of the farm of William
P. Morris, thence due east to the Pocomoke
River, thence with the channel of said river
to the beginning, the Judges of election, in
each of said Districts, shall receive the ballots
of each elector, voting at said election, who
has resided for six months, preceding said
election within said limits, for or against a
new County; and the Return Judges of said
Election Districts shall certify the result of
such voting, in the manner now prescribed
by Law, to the Governor, who shall by Proclamation make known the same; and if a
majority of the legal votes, cast within that
part of Worcester County, contained within
said lines, and also a majority of the legal
votes cast within that part of Somerset
County, contained within said lines, shall be
in favor of a new County, then said parts
of Worcester and Somerset Counties shall
become and constitute a new County, to be
called Wicomico County; and Salisbury shall
be the County Seat. And the Inhabitants
thereof shall thenceforth have and enjoy all
such rights and privileges as are held and
enjoyed by the Inhabitants of the other Counties of this State.

Governor's Proclamation.

Salisbury the County Seat.

- Sec. 3. When said new County shall have *Division of Debts and Obligations.* been so created, the Inhabitants thereof shall cease to have any claim to, or interest in the county buildings, and other public property of every description, belonging to said Counties of Somerset and Worcester, respectively, and shall be liable for their proportionate shares of the then existing debts and obligations of the said Counties, according to the last assessment in said Counties, to be ascertained and apportioned by the Circuit Court of Somerset County, as to the debts and obligations of said County, and by the Circuit Court of Worcester County, as to the debts and obligations of Worcester County, on the petition of the County Commissioners of the said Counties, respectively; and the property in each part of the said Counties, included in said new County, shall be bound only for the share of the debts and obligations of the county from which it shall be separated; and the Inhabitants of said new county shall also pay the County taxes, levied upon *Taxes.* them at the time of the creation of such new County, as if such new County had not been created; and on the application of twelve citizens of the proposed county of Wicomico, the Surveyor of Worcester County shall run and locate the line from Meadow Bridge to the Pocomoke River, previous to the adoption, or rejection of this Constitution, and at the expense of said petitioners.

8

SEC. 4. At the first general election, held under this Constitution, the qualified voters of said new County shall be entitled to elect a Senator, and two Delegates to the General. Assembly, and all such County, or other officers as this Constitution may authorize, or require to be elected by other Counties of the State; a notice of such election shall be given by the Sheriffs of Worcester and Somerset Counties in the manner now prescribed by Law; and in case said new County shall be established, as aforesaid, then the Counties of Somerset and Worcester shall be entitled to elect but two Delegates each to the General Assembly.

SEC. 5. The County of Wicomico, if formed according to the provisions of this Constitution, shall be embraced in the First Judicial Circuit; and the times for holding the Courts therein shall be fixed and determined by the General Assembly.

General Assembly to carry
this Art. into
effect.

SEC. 6. The General Assembly shall pass all such Laws as may be necessary more fully to carry into effect the provisions of this Article.

ARTICLE XIV.

AMENDMENTS TO THE CONSTITUTION.

SECTION 1. The General Assembly may propose Amendments to this Constitution; provided, that each Amendment shall be embraced in a separate Bill, embodying the Article or Section, as the same will stand when amended and passed by three-fifths of all the members elected to each of the two Houses, by yeas and nays, to be entered on the Journals with the proposed Amendment. The Bill, or Bills, proposing amendment, or amendments, shall be published by order of the Governor, in at least two newspapers in each county, where so many may be published, and where not more than one may be published, then in that newspaper, and in three newspapers published in the City of Baltimore, one of which shall be in the German language, once a week, for at least three months preceding the next ensuing general election, at which the said proposed amendment, or amendments shall be submitted, in a form to be prescribed by the General Assembly, to the qualified voters of the State for adoption or rejection. The votes cast for and against said proposed amendment, or

General Assembly may propose amendments, to be passed by three-fifths of each house.

Publication in Newspapers

Submission to voters.

Returns to
Governor.
amendments, severally, shall be returned to
the Governor, in the manner prescribed in
other cases, and if it shall appear to the
Governor that a majority of the votes cast at
said election on said amendment, or amendments, severally, were cast in favor thereof,
Proclamation
of Governor.
the Governor shall, by his Proclamation, declare the said amendment, or amendments,
having received said majority of votes, to
have been adopted by the People of Maryland as part of the Constitution thereof, and
thenceforth said amendment, or amendments
shall be part of the said Constitution. When
Each Amend-
ment to be
voted on sepa-
rately.
two or more amendments shall be submitted,
in manner aforesaid, to the voters of this
State at the same election, they shall be so
submitted as that each amendment shall be
voted on separately.

Convention
every 20 years.
1858, c. 255.
SEC. 2. It shall be the duty of the General
Assembly to provide by Law for taking, at
the general election to be held in the year
eighteen hundred and eighty-seven, and every
twenty years thereafter, the sense of the People in regard to calling a Convention for
altering this Constitution; and if a majority
of voters at such election or elections shall
vote for a Convention, the General Assembly,
at its next session, shall provide by Law
for the assembling of such Convention, and
for the election of Delegates thereto. Each
County, and Legislative District of the City

of Baltimore, shall have in such Convention a number of Delegates equal to its represen- No. of Delegates. tation in both Houses at the time at which the Convention is called. But any Constitution, or change, or amendment of the existing Constitution, which may be adopted by such Convention, shall be submitted to the Submission to voters. voters of this State, and shall have no effect unless the same shall have been adopted by a majority of the voters voting thereon.

MISCELLANEOUS.

ARTICLE XV.

SECTION 1. Every person holding any office Returns of created by, or existing under the Constitution, Fees to be made annually, or Laws of the State, (except Justices of the to the Comptroller. Peace, Constables and Coroners,) or holding 1853, c. 444. 1854, c. 196. any appointment under any Court of this State, whose pay, or compensation is derived from fees, or moneys coming into his hands for the discharge of his official duties; or, in any way, growing out of, or connected with his office, shall keep a book in which shall be entered every sum, or sums of money, received by him, or on his account, as a payment or compensation for his performance of official duties, a copy of which entries in said book, verified by the oath of the officer, by whom it is directed to be kept, shall be returned yearly to the Comptroller of the State for his inspection, and that of the General Assembly of the State, to which the Comptroller shall, at each regular session thereof, make a report showing what officers have complied with this Section; and each of the said officers, when the amount received by him for the year shall exceed the sum which he is by Law entitled to retain, as his salary, or compensation for the discharge of his duties, and for the expenses of his office, shall yearly pay over to the Treasurer of the State

Excess over Salary to be paid over.

the amount of such excess, subject to such disposition thereof as the General Assembly

On failure for 30 days Governor to declare office vacant.

may direct; if any of such officers shall fail to comply with the requisitions of this Section for the period of thirty days after the expiration of each and every year of his office, such officer shall be deemed to have vacated his office, and the Governor shall declare the same vacant, and the vacancy therein shall be filled as in case of vacancy for any other cause, and such officer shall be subject to suit by the State for the amount that ought to be paid into the Treasury; and no person holding any office created by, or existing under this Constitution, or Laws of the State, or holding any appointment, under any Court in this State, shall receive more than three thousand dollars a year as a compensation for the discharge of his official duties, except in cases specially provided in this Constitution. *Salaries limited to $3,000.*

SEC. 2. The several Courts existing in this State at the time of the adoption of this Constitution, shall, until superseded under its provisions, continue with like powers and jurisdiction, and in the exercise thereof, both at Law and in Equity, in all respects, as if this Constitution had not been adopted; and when said Courts shall be so superseded, all causes, then depending in said Courts, shall pass into the jurisdiction of the several Courts, by which they may, [be] respectively, superseded. *The Courts to continue until superseded.*

SEC. 3. The Governor, and all officers, civil and military, now holding office under this State, whether by election, or appointment, shall continue to hold, exercise and discharge the duties of their offices (unless inconsistent with, or otherwise provided in this Constitution) until they shall be superseded, under its provisions, and until their successors shall be duly qualified. *Governor and all officers to hold office until superseded.*

SEC. 4. If at any election directed by this Constitution, any two or more candidates shall have the highest and an equal number *New election in case of tie. 1854, c. 26.*

of votes, a new election shall be ordered by the Governor, except in cases specially provided for by this Constitution.

Jury judges of law and fact. 12 Md. 236; 22 Md. 386.

Sec. 5. In the trial of all criminal cases, the Jury shall be the Judges of Law, as well as of fact.

Right of trial by Jury.

Sec. 6. The right of trial by Jury of all issues of fact in civil proceedings in the several Courts of Law in this State, where the amount in controversy exceeds the sum of five dollars, shall be inviolably preserved.

General elections to be held in November.

Sec. 7. All general elections in this State shall be held on the Tuesday next after the first Monday in the month of November, in the year in which they shall occur; and the first election of all officers, who, under this Constitution, are required to be elected by the People, shall, except in cases herein specially provided for, be held on the Tuesday next after the first Monday of November, in the year eighteen hundred and sixty-seven.

Sheriffs to give notice of elections.

Sec. 8. The Sheriffs of the several Counties of this State, and of the City of Baltimore, shall give notice of the several elections authorized by this Constitution, in the manner prescribed by existing Laws for elections to be held in this State, until said Laws shall be changed.

Terms of office to commence from election.

Sec. 9. The Term of office of all Judges and other officers, for whose election provi-

sion is made by this Constitution, shall ex- Exceptions.
cept in cases otherwise expressly provided
herein, commence from the time of their Election; and all such officers shall qualify as
soon after their election as practicable, and
shall enter upon the duties of their respective
offices immediately upon their qualification;
and the Term of office of the State Librarian
and of the Commissioner of the Land Office
shall commence from the time of their appointment.

SEC. 10. Any officer elected or appointed How officers
in pursuance of the provisions of this Con- may qualify.
stitution, may qualify, either according to
the existing provisions of Law, in relation
to officers under the present Constitution, or
before the Governor of the State, or before
any Clerk of any Court of Record in any
part of the State; but in case an officer shall ·
qualify out of the County in which he resides,
an official copy of his oath shall be filed and Copy of oath to
recorded in the Clerk's office of the Circuit be recorded.
Court of the County in which he may reside,
or in the Clerk's office of the Superior Court
of the City of Baltimore, if he shall reside
therein.

Vote on the Constitution.

Governor's Proclamation directing Sheriffs to give notice of election on this Constitution.

For the purpose of ascertaining the sense of the people of this State, in regard to the adoption, or rejection of this Constitution, the Governor shall issue his Proclamation within five days after the adjournment of this Convention, directed to the Sheriffs of the City of Baltimore, and of the several Counties of this State, commanding them to give notice, in the manner now prescribed by Law in reference to the election of members of the House of Delegates, that an election for the adoption or rejection of this Constitution, will be held in the City of Baltimore, and in the several Counties of this State, on Wednesday, the Eighteenth day of September, in the year eighteen hundred and sixty-seven, at the usual places of holding elections for members of the House of Delegates in said City and Counties. At the said election the vote shall be by ballot, and upon each ballot, there shall be written or printed the words "For the Constitution," or "Against the Constitution," as the voter may elect; and the provisions of the Laws of this State, relating to the holding of general elections for members of the House of Delegates, shall, in all respects, apply to, and regulate the holding of the said election. It shall be the duty of the Judges of Election, in said City, and in the several Counties of the State, to receive, accurately count, and duly return the number of ballots, so cast for, or against the adoption of this Constitution, as well as any blank ballots, which may be cast, to the several Clerks of the Circuit Courts of this State, and to the Clerk of the Superior Court of Baltimore City, in the manner now prescribed by Law, in reference to the election of members of the House of Delegates, and duplicates thereof directly to the Governor; and the several Clerks, aforesaid shall return to the Governor, within ten days after said election, the number of ballots cast for or against the Constitution, and the number of blank ballots; and the Governor, upon receiving the returns from the Judges of Election or the Clerks as aforesaid and ascertaining the aggregate vote throughout the State, shall, by his Proclamation, make known the same; and if a majority of the votes cast shall be for the adoption of this Constitution, it shall go into effect on Saturday, the Fifth day of October, eighteen hundred and sixty-seven.

Governor's Proclamation if Constitution adopted.

Done in Convention, the seventeenth day of August, in the year of our Lord one thousand eight hundred and sixty-seven, and of the Independence of the United States the ninety-second.

RICHD. B. CARMICHAEL,

President of the Convention.

ATTEST:

MILTON Y. KIDD,

Secretary

MARYLAND, *Sct:*

I, GEORGE EARLE, *Clerk of the Court of Appeals of Maryland, do hereby certify, that the above Constitution, was filed in the Clerk's Office of said Court, on the seventeenth day of August, in the year of our Lord one thousand eight hundred and sixty-seven.*

Witness my hand: GEORGE EARLE,

Clerk of the Court of Appeals of Maryland.

APPENDIX.

I APPEND to this edition of the Declaration of Rights and the Constitution of the State of Maryland, a brief Commentary shewing some of the principal changes which have been made in them, — and thus giving at a glance a short history of the form of Government.

An investigation into the causes of these changes is necessary to a perfect understanding of them; but there is not space in this edition for such a work. Those who wish to look more deeply into the matter are referred to the Histories of the State, and to the Debates in the Constitutional Conventions.

THE DECLARATION OF RIGHTS.

This Declaration consists principally of immutable principles of government, and these it was impossible to change, — but considerable change has been made in the phraseology of many of the Articles.

The most important changes are the result of the recent War, — and relate to Slavery, — the relations of this state to the General Government of the United States, to retrospective oaths, to forfeiture of estate for treason, and to violations of Constitutional provisions.

The First Article of the Declaration, which. was inserted for the first time in 1864 — relating to certain inalienable rights and intended, doubtless, to apply to the condition of the colored people recently freed — was omitted by the late Convention. And the original First Article is retained, with the words " according to the mode pre-scribed in this Constitution," which were inserted in 1851, — and omitted in 1864, still omitted, — leaving therefore the declaration of the right of the people, at all times, to alter their form of government " in such manner as they may deem expedient," entirely unrestricted as to the mode of its exercise.

ART. 2. Is a substitute for ART. 5 of 1864, which was entirely new at that time. It makes a great change in the mode of declaring the Constitution, &c., of the United States to be the Supreme Law, and omits the declaration of paramount allegiance to the United States.

121

ART. 3. Is new. It refers to the reserved powers of the States and People.

ART. 4. Is the same as Art. 3 in 1864, relating to this State's Rights, with the addition of the words "as a free, sovereign and independent State."

From No. 6 to No. 43, inclusive, the numbers of the Articles are the same as the Articles on similar subjects in 1864.

ART. 7. Remains as in 1851 and 1864, except that the word "free" is omitted before the words "white male citizen." Formerly the right of suffrage was restricted to those having property.

In ART. 15, the words "on persons or property," with reference to the imposition of taxes, were inserted in 1851 but are omitted in 1864 and 1867.

In ART. 17, after the declaration that no *ex post facto* law ought to be made, are the additional words, "nor any retrospective oath or restriction be imposed, or required."

In ART. 19, the word "free"—in relation to the right to have justice—is omitted in 1864 and 1867.

In ART. 23, relating to imprisonment, &c., the same omission occurs, and the provision in 1851 authorizing the Legislature to pass laws to regulate the colored people is also omitted in 1864 and in 1867.

ART. 24 substitutes for the declaration in 1864, abolishing slavery, one, that it having been abolished by the United States, it shall not be reestablished, and that compensation is due therefor from the United States.

ART. 27 was changed in 1864 so as to allow forfeiture of estate for treason. This provision has been stricken out and the Article restored to its original form, declaring that no conviction shall work forfeiture.

In ART. 31, the phraseology in regard to quartering soldiers in time of war, was changed in 1864 so that the manner of it shall be "prescribed by law," instead of "as the Legislature may direct," and so it now remains.

ART. 33 relates to the independency of Judges. This Article has undergone many changes since 1776. It was then declared with a *wherefore* that "all judges ought to hold commissions during good behaviour," and the same thing is declared in the Constitution of the United States, obviously meaning the tenure of their office for life. When in 1851 the tenure was reduced to ten years these words were omitted, and so in 1864 and 1867.

In this Article, as it originally stood, there was a declaration also that liberal salaries ought to be provided by the Legislature, but in 1851 and since, the salaries are fixed in the Constitution. The causes and manner of removal also were originally stated in this Article, and so remained in 1851 and in 1864, but the declaration now is, "that Judges shall not be removed, except in the manner, and for the causes provided in this Constitution."

ART. 36, originally provided that "all persons *professing the Christian Religion* are equally entitled to protection in their religious liberty," and also the Legislature was authorized to lay a tax for the support of the Christian Religion. And it is observable that King Charles, in the Charter of the State, names a "*zeal for extending the Christian Religion*, and also the territories of our empire," as animating the Baron of Baltimore, and the inducements to the Grant. In 1851 and since, these declarations are omitted, and further, in 1864, the word Jew is omitted, and in 1867 neither Jew nor Christian is named, nor is there any mention whatever of the Christian Religion.

ART. 37, expressly declares that "*no religious test* ought ever to be required,"—and prohibits the Legislature from prescribing any other oath than that prescribed by the Constitution,—the change being, that in 1864 reference was made to the Christian Religion and an oath of allegiance required. The original Art. 37, providing for the rights of the City of Annapolis, is omitted in 1864 and in 1867.

In ART. 38 there was inserted in 1864 a provision for the *prior or subsequent* sanction of the Legislature to gifts or devises for religious purposes and it now remains.

To ART. 40, on the Liberty of the Press, was added in 1864 an extension of the declaration to every citizen to speak, write and publish his sentiments, and a declaration of the responsibility for the abuse of that liberty was also added

ART. 43. Certain duties of the Legislature were declared in 1851, viz: to diffuse knowledge, promote the arts and sciences, &c., and in 1864 the extension of education was added and so it remains.

ART. 44, contains new declaration of the applicability of Constitutional princip.es in War and in Peace, and that a departure from them under plea of necessity tends to anarchy and despotism. The Last Article originally declared that the form of government should not be altered by the Legislature except in the manner prescribed, and this with slight variations was continued in 1851, and in 1864, but it is entirely omitted in 1867.

THE CONSTITUTION.

A great many changes have been made in the Constitution, the principal of which, are the omission of retrospective oaths of office and for the Elective Franchise;

The giving of the Veto Power to the Governor;

The abolishing of the office of Lieutenant Governor;

The making of the whole population instead of the white population the basis of representation in the lower House of the Legislature and the establishing of a different numerical ratio for such representation;

The reinstating of the clause making Ministers of the Gospel ineligible to the Legislature;

The rendering of persons of all races and colors competent witnesses;

The prohibition upon the Legislature from suspending the writ of *Habeas Corpus;*

The authorizing of a change in the legal rate of interest by the Legislature;

The abolishing of the office of Pension Commissioner;

The entire change of the Judicial system by providing for eight Judicial Circuits instead of thirteen, with three Judges for each instead of one for each, and the constituting the eight Chief Justices of the Circuits the Court of Appeals—instead of an independent Court of five Judges,—so that the Judges of the Court of Appeals are elected by the people of each Circuit, respectively, instead of by the people of the whole State;

The requiring that all cases in Court of Appeals stand for hearing at the first term, instead of certain special cases only;

The making the Clerk of the Court of Appeals eligible by the People, instead of to be appointed by the Court;

The direction to the Court of Appeals to frame rules in Equity;

The increase of the salaries of all the Judges in the State, except those of the Orphans' Courts;

The union of the five Judges of the several Courts in Baltimore City into an additional Court, called the Supreme Bench, having some supervisory powers in the nature of appeals, without, however, restricting the right of appeal to the Court of Appeals, as heretofore, and the assignment of the several Judges from time to time to their respective Courts,—and the giving of concurrent jurisdiction in all common law cases to each of three several Courts;

The change of the terms of office of the Judges of the Orphans' Court from six to four years, and making the terms all expire together instead of one every two years, as heretofore;

The change of the term of office of the County Commissioners from four to two years;

The provision for a change by the Legislature of the present system of Education.

These and some minor changes will more fully appear by a careful comparison of the two forms of Government by Articles and Sections, as follows:

ARTICLE I.—ELECTIVE FRANCHISE.

SECTION 1. Requires a residence in the State one year, and six months residence in the legislative district or the county in which one votes. The phraseology of this section differs considerably from that of both 1851 and 1864, and may vary the rights of voters on the question of residence.

SEC. 2. Requires again that lunatics shall be under guardianship before being disfranchised, a provision inserted in 1851 but omitted in 1864.

SEC. 5. Provides for Registration and makes it conclusive evidence of the right to vote.

SEC. 6. Containing the oath of office provides simply for the support of the Constitution of the United States and of this State, and to execute the office and not to receive profits of any other office, omitting entirely the retrospective clauses and references to the late rebellion inserted in 1864, and omitting also the oath against bribery inserted in 1851 and continued in 1864.

ARTICLE II.—EXECUTIVE DEPARTMENT.

SECTION 1. The term of office of the Governor was changed from three to four years in 1851, and it so remains. By this change the expiration of it is made to coincide with every second term of the Delegates, they being elected biennially, in which respect there is a similarity between the Constitution of this State and that of the United States. Under the Constitution of 1864,—the elections were held in that year and every four years thereafter, but now in 1867 and every four years thereafter,—thus the elections for Governor are now held the year before the Presidential elections instead of in the same year, and so the Elections for Delegates are held in the years intervening between those for Congressmen, instead of in the same years

9

In 1851 the State was divided into three Gubernatorial districts, from each of which the Governor was chosen in rotation, whence it resulted that the same man could not be chosen Governor until after the expiration of eight years; this provision was omitted in 1864 and in 1867.

The provision for a Lieutenant Governor, inserted in 1864, is omitted in 1867.

SEC. 3. Provides that the person having the highest number of votes shall be the Governor—thus not requiring a majority of the whole but a plurality only.

And by SEC. 4 it is provided that when two or more persons have the highest and an equal number of votes for Governor, the second vote shall be confined to those persons, and if the votes be again · equal, the election is to be determined by lot. The great use of such a provision, in some cases, will readily be perceived by those who have studied the history of the elections of Speakers, Presidents and other officers, both in the National and State Legislatures.

The plan of continually dropping the lowest candidate is often practiced on, with advantage—but 'if at last there be a tie, the decision by lot is the simplest and best on many accounts.

SEC. 5. Requires the Governor to have been ten years a citizen and five years a resident of Maryland. In 1851 and in 1864 it was five years a citizen of the United States and five years a resident of this State.

SECS. 6 and 7. Provide for the election of a new Governor by the General Assembly in case of vacancy and the filling of that office, by the President of Senate or Speaker of House during its recess, which provisions are the same as in 1851 and were necessarily reinstated upon abolishing the office of Lieutenant Governor.

SEC. 8. The prohibition of the Governor from taking the command in person of the forces of the State without the consent of the Legislature, inserted in 1851 and 1864, is continued.

SEC. 17. The most important change of all concerning the Executive office, is investing it with the Veto Power.

The words in which this power is given are nearly the same as in the Constitution of the United States. There is, however, a preamble prefixed defining its use to be "to guard against hasty or partial legislation, and encroachments of the Legislative Department upon the co-ordinate Executive and Judicial Departments,"—and three-fifths of each branch may pass bills over the veto instead of as in the U. S. two-thirds.

SEC. 18. The duty of the Governor to examine the books of the Treasurer and Comptroller, imposed in 1851 and continued in 1864, is continued in 1867, with the further duty of examining both of those officers under oath.

SEC. 20. The restrictions upon the pardoning power, imposed in 1851, are continued.

SEC. 21. The salary in 1851 was $3,600—in 1864, $4,000, and now, $4,500.

SECS. 22 and 23. The salary of the Secretary of State, fixed at $1,000 in 1851 and so continued in 1864, is now $2,000, and the office of Private Secretary ceases and the Secretary of State performs all the clerical duty belonging to the Executive Department.

In 1851, the Governor's office was stripped of its important prerogative of appointing Judges and many other officers, by and with the advice and consent of the Senate, and these changes have been since retained.

ARTICLE III.—LEGISLATIVE DEPARTMENT.

SECTION 2. In 1851,— the term of office of Senators was reduced from six to four years, and by a subsequent section it is provided that one half of them, instead of one-third, as formerly, should be elected biennially, and these provisions remain. The Constitution, prior to 1851, was like that of the United States.

In 1864,— the city of Baltimore was divided into three districts, each entitled to one Senator, and this provision remains; before that time the city was entitled to one Senator only.

SECS. 3 and 4. In 1851,— for the first time, the principle of representation according to population was adopted; but Baltimore city was restricted to four more than the largest county, by which rule it was entitled to ten members.

In 1864,— the principle of representation according to population was applied by a peculiar and artificial rule, limiting the larger counties and the city of Baltimore, but giving as a result, a larger representation than heretofore to that city— that is, six members to each of its three Legislative Districts. In 1867, another rule or sliding scale was adopted, based somewhat upon the principle of representation according to population, but still limiting the city of Baltimore and the larger counties—the result being the same to Baltimore city, viz : that it now has eighteen members ; but this number may be increased by the results of each succeeding census.

Before 1851, the basis of representation was the same as in the United States; that is, it embraced three-fifths of the colored population. In 1851, the whole population was made the basis. In 1864, the white population was made the basis. In 1867, the whole population is again made the basis. The result of adopting this latter basis is to give the smaller counties, in which there is a larger ratio of colored people, a larger representation in the House of Delegates.

SECS. 6 and 7. In 1851,—the election of Delegates, and of one-half of the Senators, and the Sessions of the Legislature, were made biennial, and they have since so remained.

The elections of Representatives in Congress are biennial, but the Sessions of that body annual.

The elections for Senators and Delegates in Maryland are held in the years intervening between those in which the elections for representatives in Congress are held.

SEC. 11. The provision making Ministers of the Gospel ineligible, which was omitted in 1864, is now reinstated.

SECS. 14 and 15. The Legislature prior to 1851, met in December. In 1851 the first Wednesday in January was made the commencement of its sessions and so it remains. In 1851 the 10th day of March was made the end of the sessions, but in 1864 the session was unlimited, but no member was allowed to receive more than $400— the per diem being $5.00 instead of $4.00—equal to 80 working days. In 1867 the per diem remains the same and the mileage is not to exceed 20 cents per mile, and the sessions are to be "for a period not longer than 90 days."

SEC. 27. Prior to 1851 the Senate could not originate money bills,—in 1851 this restriction was taken away and so it remains. In 1851 it was provided that no bill should originate in the last three days of the session,—in 1864 this restriction was made ten days and so it remains; and the provisions for reading bills on three several days, adopted in 1851, are retained.

SEC. 29. In 1851 provision was made for codification of the laws of the State and the code was adopted in 1860, and the amendments since made are enacted as the law would read when amended.

SEC. 33. In 1851 the Legislature was prohibited from granting divorces, and in 1864 the prohibition was extended so as to embrace local or special laws on many subjects, and these useful restrictions are continued in 1867.

SEC. 34. In 1851,—it was provided that the State should not create any debt without providing taxes for its payment in 15 years and for the payment of interest on it annually, or lend the credit of the State, but the State might borrow $50,000 to meet temporary deficiencies. These useful restrictions have been since continued, but in 1867 it is allowed to appropriate not more than $500,000 to Internal Improvements in St. Mary's, Charles and Calvert counties.

SEC. 37. In 1864,—the Legislature was prohibited from paying for emancipated slaves, and so it is in 1867—but measures may be adopted to obtain pay for them from the United States.

SECS. 38, 43 and 44. The abolishment of imprisonment for debt, the protection of a wife's property, and the exemption of a certain amount of a debtor's property, in 1851, remain.

SEC 48. Provides for a revision of the laws relating to Corporations.

SEC. 49. Provides for punishment for bribery and for compelling persons bribing to testify against those bribed.

SEC. 51. Provides for taxation in the city or county where a person resides the greater part of the year; but for the taxation of goods where they are permanently located.

SEC. 53. Makes no person incompetent as a witness on account of race or color.

SEC. 55. Prohibits the Legislature from suspending the writ of *Habeas Corpus.*

SEC. 57. Allows the Legislature to provide for more than six per cent. interest.

ARTICLE IV.—JUDICIARY DEPARTMENT.

In 1851,—great changes were made in this department,—among which were the substitution of a tenure for a term of years, for the life tenure of the Judges; the election by the people of Judges, Clerks, Registers, Justices of the Peace, Constables and Attorneys of the State; the substitution of one Judge for three in the inferior Courts of Common Law and Equity; the abolishment of the Court of Chancery; and the establishment of a Court of Appeals, composed of four Judges, entirely independent of the inferior Courts.

SEC. 3. In 1851,—the term of office of the Judges of all except the Orphans' Courts was 10 years; in 1864 it was lengthened to 15 years, and so it remains. The term was in 1851 also limited to 70 years of age, and this restriction remains, modified however by a clause allowing the Legislature to extend the term beyond 70. To this section is added a clause allowing removals by the Legislature upon vote of two-thirds, on account of sickness or infirmity.

SEC. 8. Authorizes the parties to have a cause tried without a Jury.

SEC. 10. Gives power to the Judges to see that the duties of the Clerks are faithfully performed, and also to make rules for the government of the Clerks.

SEC. 14. In 1851 the Court of Appeals consisted of *four* judges and in 1864 of *five*, and they were chosen separately from the judges of the inferior Courts, and the duties of the Judges of the Court of Appeals were independent of those of the inferior Courts. Now the Court of Appeals is constituted of eight judges, viz : the seven Chief Judges of seven of the Judicial Circuits and an additional Judge for this Court from Baltimore City. The jurisdiction of this Court in 1851 was appellate only, and in 1864 the jurisdiction is to be prescribed by law, and so it remains, and in 1864 the sessions of this Court were fixed for first Monday in April and October or as might be directed by law, and so it remains.

SEC. 15. *Four* Judges of this Court constitute a quorum, but no cause can be decided without *three* concurring, and the Judge who heard the cause below does not sit, and all cases stand for hearing at first term.

SEC. 17. The election of the Clerk of the Court of Appeals by the people is a change, as in 1851 and in 1864 he was appointed by the Court.

SEC. 18. Contains some excellent provisions requiring the Court of Appeals to make rules on several important matters, such as the time and manner of taking appeals, the record, the practice, costs and fees, and rules in Equity.

SEC. 19. Divides the State into eight Judicial Circuits.

SEC. 20. Requires that a Court be held in each county, to be styled the Circuit Court for the County.

SEC. 21. Gives a Chief and two Associate Judges to each Circuit, and provides that no two of the Associates shall reside in the same county. Two jury terms are to be held in each county every year and two intermediate terms, and special terms may be held at any time, and one Judge may transact any business.

SEC. 22. Provides for motions in *banc* before all three Judges.

SEC. 24. The salaries of Judges of the Court of Appeals in 1851 was $2,500, in 1864 $3,000, and now $3,500,—and of the Circuit Courts in 1851 $2,000 and in 1864 $2,500, and now $2,800 ; and of the Courts in Baltimore in 1851 $2,500 and in 1864 $3,000, and now it is $3,500, but the City Council may add $500 more.

SEC. 27, &c. The arrangement of the Courts in Baltimore is new and peculiar, six Courts are provided for. The Supreme Bench is composed of one Chief and four Associate Judges, and this Court is required to assign one or more of their number to each of the other five Courts and to provide for the sickness or absence of any Judge.

SEC. 33. This Court is required to hold general terms, to make rules for each of the Courts and to hear motions for new trial, &c., but the right of appeal is reserved.

SEC. 39. Provision is made for another Court in Baltimore City and also for changing the jurisdiction of the several Courts in Baltimore City.

SEC. 40. The Judges of the Orphans' Court in 1851 were elected for four years and in 1864 the term was enlarged to six years and one Judge was chosen every two years, now the term is reduced to four years, and all are elected together as in 1851.

SEC. 42. Justices of the Peace and Constables were in 1851 elected by the people ;—but in 1864 a return was made to the appointments of the Justices of the Peace by the Governor, with the advice and consent of the Senate, and of Constables by the County Commissioners and Mayor and City Council, and so it remains.

SEC. 44. In 1851,—two persons were voted for as Sheriffs, and in 1864 this was changed and one only chosen, and so it remains.

ARTICLE V.—ATTORNEY GENERAL, &C.

SECTION 1. In 1851,—the office of Attorney General was abolished, and his Deputies who had before that time been appointed, were, under the name of State's Attorneys, chosen by the People.

In 1864,—the office of Attorney General was reestablished, and he is chosen for four years by the people, and so are all the State's Attorneys.

ARTICLE VI.—TREASURY DEPARTMENT.

In 1851,—the whole of this Department was remodeled. The Comptroller of the Treasury, a new officer, was set up to check the Treasurer. The former is elected by the people and the latter by the Legislature.

This plan of giving authority to one from one source and to the other from another source makes them, in a measure independent of each other, and thereby the danger of collusion is greatly lessened.

By the old system there was no such check upon the Treasurer, the integrity of a single individual being the chief and almost the only safeguard of the State in regard to its treasure. The provisions adopted in 1851 remain substantially the same; it is to be noted however that the Governor is required to examine both of these officers under oath as well as their books.

ARTICLE VII. — SUNDRY OFFICES.

SEC. 3. Provides for the appointment of State Librarian by the Governor, with the advice and consent of the Senate, and for a law defining his duties. In 1864 he was chosen by the Legislature.

ARTICLE VIII. — EDUCATION.

This Article requires the Legislature at its first Session to adopt a thorough and efficient system of Free Public Schools and to provide for their maintenance, — and for the expiration of the present system adopted in 1851.

ARTICLE IX. — MILITIA.

In 1851 a Militia system was provided for and certain officers were to be elected by the companies, &c., and an Adjutant General was to be appointed by the Governor, by and with the advice and consent of the Senate, for six years.

In 1864 the Militia were defined to be citizens between 18 and 45 years of age, but the provisions for electing officers were omitted, and the Adjutant was to hold office during the pleasure of the Governor.

In 1867 the Legislature is required to pass laws concerning the Militia, no provision being contained in this Article, except for an Adjutant, and his term of office is not defined otherwise than that " he shall hold his office until the appointment and qualification of his successor, or until removed in pursuance of a Court Martial."

ARTICLE X. — LABOR AND AGRICULTURE.

This is a new Article and provides for a Superintendent of Labor and Agriculture, to be elected by the people for four years.

ARTICLE XI.— CITY OF BALTIMORE.

SEC. 1. This is a new Article. The Mayor is elected for four years and is ineligible for the second term.

SEC. 2. The City Council is divided into two Branches.

SEC. 3. The First Branch is elected every year and the Second every two years.

SEC. 4. The regular sessions are to continue not more than ninety days and the extra sessions not more than twenty days

SEC. 5. The members are not to hold any other offices nor to be interested in any City contracts.

SEC. 6. The Mayor may be removed on conviction in a Court of Law.

SEC. 7. No debt can be created nor can the credit of the city be lent, unless authorized by the Legislature and approved by a vote of the people.

SECS. 8 and 9. Authorizes the Legislature to change any part of this Article, except the seventh section.

ARTICLE XII. — PUBLIC WORKS.

Some of the provisions of this Article are new, and the Board is authorized to sell or exchange the State's interest in some of the works of Internal Improvement.

ARTICLE XIII. — NEW COUNTIES.

By this Article the new county of Wicomico is created out of parts of Somerset and Worcester, and provision is made for other new counties to be created under authority of the Legislature.

ARTICLE XIV. — AMENDMENTS TO THE CONSTITUTION.

In 1851 the only method of amendment provided was by a Convention to be called by the Legislature, upon taking the sense of the people after every census. Before that time amendments were made by Act of the Legislature, passed at one session and confirmed at the next. In 1864 three modes of amendment were provided, viz: first, three-fifths of both houses were authorized to propose amendments to the people; secondly, two-thirds of both houses were authorized to call a Convention, and, thirdly, in 1882, and in every twentieth year thereafter, the question of a Convention was to be put to the people.

Now, the plan of submitting Amendments to the People by three fifths of each House is retained—and also the plan of submitting to the People, every twenty years, the question of calling a Convention; but the Legislature is not by this Article as it now stands expressly authorized to call a Convention, or even to submit the question of a call to the People at any other time.

ARTICLE XV.—MISCELLANEOUS.

This Article provides for returns of excesses of fees by all officers; the continuance of the Courts, and all officers until superseded; for new elections in cases of tie; that Juries be judges of law and fact in criminal cases, and for Jury trials; and fixes the terms of office of all officers in the State more definitely than heretofore.

THE VOTE ON THE CONSTITUTION

and the Proclamation of the Governor thereupon are provided for at the conclusion of the Constitution.

CONCLUSION.

The Legislature is directed by this Constitution to pass laws on several subjects, particularly pointed out, in order to carry out its provisions, and to conform to the changes made.·

The author of these brief notes hopes that they may prove an acceptable guide to the study of some questions of the Constitutional History of this State,—and particularly as to the changes recently made.

EDWARD OTIS HINKLEY.

BALTIMORE, *Oct.* 23rd, 1867.

INDEX.

NOTE.— In this Index those Articles to which no Section is added, are in the Declaration of Rights: the Articles in the Constitution being followed by their Sections.

10

146 INDEX.

11

INDEX. **151**